THE
MILLIONAIRE
CODES

*The Secret Brain Science Path
to Supernatural Success*

SUZANNE LONGSTREET
& SARA CONNELL

The Millionaire Codes

Copyright © 2025 Suzanne Longstreet & Sara Connell

Cover design by Claudine Mansour Design. Interior design by Michael Beas.

Disclaimer: The following is for informational and entertainment purposes only and should not be considered financial or health advice. Readers are responsible for their mental and physical health and choices. Always consult with a financial advisor and mental health professional before making important decisions. Some names and distinguishing characteristics of individuals and organizations represented in this book have been changed to respect confidentiality. While best efforts have been made in preparing this book, the author and publisher make no warranty, representation, or guarantee with respect to the accuracy or completeness of information contained herein.

Published by Thought Leader Academy Publishing
3901 North Kildare Ave
Chicago, IL | 60641

Paperback ISBN: 979-8-9922572-3-6

Table of Contents

Part One: Introduction & Mission

Part Two: Welcome to the World of NLP

Part Three: The Millionaire Codes

We're absolutely thrilled you're joining us on this transformational journey.

The Millionaire Codes were designed to unlock the next level of your success, abundance, and impact. As you explore the codes, you might find yourself wondering how to fully embody and integrate them into your life and business. That's where we come in.

We've shared a series of videos to guide you through each code—so you can experience the shifts in real time, with us by your side.

Plus, you'll get access to powerful bonus resources, all designed to support you in stepping into the visionary leader you're meant to be.

Access the codes and your free bonus resources anytime, https://millionaire.codes

The codes are here. Your vision is waiting. Let's ignite it—together.

Part One:
Introduction & Mission

You hold in your hands an invitation—a portal to a completely new reality. It's no coincidence that you're here. You called this book into your life because you're ready. Ready for a breakthrough. Ready to shatter your next glass ceiling. Ready to *RISE*.

What are the Millionaire Codes? How do they work? That's exactly what you're about to discover. And more importantly, you're going to *ACTIVATE* them. This isn't just about learning—it's about stepping into the wealth, success, and power that has always been waiting for you.

Sara's Commitment to Reach $1 Million

The year I first committed to making $1 million in my business, I did what I always do when I set a big goal: I got into *research mode*. I sought out individuals who had already achieved what I wanted to accomplish—people who inspired me and whose values aligned with mine—and I looked for the common threads. What were the things *all* of them were doing that led to their success?

One of the first people I talked with was a coach making $5 million a year. I expected her to share a secret strategy or groundbreaking tactic, but instead, she told me something I'll never forget: the turning point for her wasn't about strategy. It was about *mindset*. She sat down and wrote a list of every limiting belief she had about making a million dollars (or more) a year. Then, she took that list to a mindset expert and cleared every single one of those beliefs from her subconscious mind. That's when everything changed for her.

Later, I met another coach who was running an 8-figure ($10 million+) business. I remember thinking, *Who are these people? Were they born with some kind of "prosperity gene?"* But when I asked about his secret, his answer was almost identical. He told me he'd been stuck at $2 million for years, spinning his wheels. The breakthrough came when he shifted his entire focus to mindset. That year, he invested over $1 million working with a mindset expert, and it paid off. He broke through the $10 million mark and has maintained (and surpassed) that ever since. "It's the most important investment I've ever made," he told me.

As I continued my research, I heard the same story over and over again from seven- and eight-figure entrepreneurs. Each time, the lesson was clear: mindset wasn't just part of their success—it was the foundation. That's when I knew this kind of work—subconscious clearing, rewiring the brain, and aligning my thoughts with success— would be *pivotal* for my journey, too.

So, I went all in. I worked with experts in Neuro-Linguistic Programming (NLP), Emotional Freedom Technique (EFT), Hypnosis, the Body Code, and other quantum modalities. And not only did this work fast-track me to a $1 million+ per year business, but it also sparked a deep fascination with the subconscious mind and the science of epigenetics.

You've probably heard the phrase, "Success leaves clues." I decided to follow those clues—and what I discovered transformed my life and my business. Now I know this: wealth isn't about being born with a special "gene." It's about clearing what's holding you back, rewiring your brain for abundance, and aligning your subconscious mind with what you want to achieve. If it worked for them—and it worked for me—it can work for you, too.

You may not have had the opportunity to work with a mindset expert one to one, or you may have wondered if it would work for you. This is why we're bringing the codes to you in this book.

This book isn't just for women, although we share a deep passion for supporting women in breaking out of the confidence gap, the pay gap, and epidemic experience of imposter syndrome and undervaluing that so many of us face.

Despite much progress in women's equality over the past thirty years, women are often still not charging or receiving what they are worth! White women make 0.75 to 0.80 every dollar made by a man. Women of color make 0.60 to every male dollar earned. This is despite women being responsible for creating more jobs and economic growth in 2023. The income gap is not just in corporate jobs and big companies. FreshBooks released a study last year that showed women freelancers (who set their own rates) made 28% less than their equivalent male counterparts. And we've continued to face challenges. Women globally lost $800 billion in income during the 2020 year of the pandemic alone! (Source: OXFAM International, April 29, 2021).

The complete answer to these gaps is not just policy change. We believe and have seen with full certainty in our own lives, and those of our clients, that just like those 7 and 8 figure entrepreneurs I talked to in my research phase, doing the brain science based subconscious reprogramming and activation work is the vital key to our individual and collective wealth rise.

Now, after many years of research, testing, working with our clients in the field we've distilled and channeled the very best of the mindset modalities, sequences, techniques into the 10 Millionaire Codes in this book.

Who Are We?

Suzanne is the founder of Success & Clarity where she coaches entrepreneurs, mostly women, to rewire their brain for success and become millionaire business owners.

Sara is the founder of Thought Leader Academy where she helps coaches, experts, and entrepreneurs become bestselling authors, in demand speakers, and to monetize their missions as they rise to world changing thought leaders.

Between us, we are trained in: Neuro Linguistic Programming (NLP), Akashic Records, Hypnosis, Automatic Writing, Meditation, TimeLine Therapy ™ Techniques, Neuroscience, Shamanic Healing, Positive Intelligence, and more. The codes combine NLP, with quantum techniques, visualization and methods we've uniquely developed over the past combined 40 years of work with clients in the field. The codes work fast. In our experience, when something shifts, it stays shifted. Suzanne has spent years learning, teaching and coaching NLP and has reached the distinction of NLP Trainer, NLP Master Coach & Master Hypnotherapist and continuously furthers her education in the field.

I believe so strongly in the subconscious clearing and alignment work that I teach it as part of the curriculum in Thought Leader Academy where I've had the gift of coaching thousands of mission-driven amazing coaches, experts and business owners to write books, speak on stages and podcasts, monetize their missions and make an undeniable positive impact on the planet.

We're so excited for what will come when you utilize these codes. This is now your, on demand, secret toolkit of our new, potent and transformation practices we've used personally and tested and used with thousands of leaders. Our intention is that you experience immediate uplevelling each time you use one of the sequences.

The Millionaire Codes are not just about money. When we unblock ourselves, we rise every aspect of our lives: self-worth, confidence, income, impact and success.

You deserve better than spending one more day letting limiting beliefs, past trauma, fear of rejection or disappointment hold you back from being the ultimate leader and from the abundance you came here to be and have. You were designed for abundance. You are a MIRACULOUS being infused with Genius which essentially means you have the power of a superhero. It's time for you to easily and consistently tap into your greatness.

How To Use This Book

In the first part of this book, you'll read about our personal stories—the highs, the lows, and the breakthrough moments that helped us shatter glass ceilings and discover what we now call the Millionaire Codes. Part I is all about the journey that brought us here.

Then, in Part II, we're going to geek out together. Suzanne loves to share about the magic of NLP. You'll learn how your brain is wired, why it sometimes feels like it's working against you, and—most importantly—how to rewire it for abundance, self-worth, and wealth creation. This is the juicy neuroscience stuff that changes everything.

In Part III is where the magic happens. You're not just going to learn about the 10 Millionaire Codes—you're going to ACTIVATE them. By the end of this part, you'll have tools you can use to create real results in your life. Oh, and we threw in a handy Glossary at the end to make all the technical stuff easier to reference.

Here's something you'll notice as you read: throughout the book, Sara uses the term "subconscious," while Suzanne uses "unconscious mind." These words might sound different, but they're talking about the same thing: the part of your mind that operates below the surface of your awareness. It's where habits, beliefs, and patterns live— basically, the operating system running the show. Whether we call it subconscious or unconscious, it's where the rewiring magic happens. So, don't get hung up on the language. Just focus on what it means for *you*.

Now, let's talk about the fact that this is a co-authored book. Two voices. Two perspectives. Two histories. We didn't try to mash them together into one. Instead, we leaned into our unique styles to give you a richer, more dynamic experience. When it's clear one of us is talking, you'll know. When we're speaking as "we," it's because we're completely aligned on what we're saying.

Bottom line: You've got two millionaire coaches here, guiding you step by step. This book is your roadmap to the Millionaire Codes— and it's designed to make your results as incredible as your potential.

Ready? Let's go!

Real People, Real Results

Within these pages, you'll hear real stories of people who didn't just dream of changing their lives—they *did it*. Using NLP techniques and processes, they transformed their businesses, relationships, and mindsets. These aren't just feel-good stories; they're proof of what's possible when you take control of your thoughts and tap into the incredible potential already inside you.

This book isn't about turning you into a certified NLP expert. It's here to wake you up, to shift how you think about your mind, and to show you how to start using it as a tool to create the results you want. We're handing you practical, proven tools to rewire your brain for success, abundance, and confidence.

We're not here to overload you with jargon or techniques. What we *are* here to do is give you the tools to create the life and business you've been dreaming of—one with more freedom, fulfillment, and success. We believe deeply in your potential, and if you're reading this, chances are, you're ready to start believing in it, too.

Let's get real for a second: you don't have to figure this out alone. While this book is a powerful starting point, the most profound transformations happen when you work with a trained and certified NLP practitioner or coach. They can guide you, help you uncover the deep-rooted beliefs holding you back, and accelerate your results.

And here's the deal: while the techniques in this book are powerful, they're not a magic wand. If you're ready for the kind of breakthrough that transforms your life, combine these tools with the support of an experienced coach. When you do, there's no limit to what you can achieve.

So, buckle up. It's time to stop holding yourself back and start stepping into the life you're meant to live.

Disclaimer: Harness Your Power with Intention

The techniques in this book are powerful, transformative tools that can help you step into the fullest expression of who you truly are. Rooted in Neuro-Linguistic Programming (NLP), these methods are designed to help you rewrite the narratives that no longer serve you, embrace your highest potential, and create a life that feels aligned and abundant.

But here's the truth: with great power comes great responsibility. The work you're about to do isn't just about achieving success; it's about doing so with integrity, compassion, and mindfulness. Your journey will not only impact you but will ripple outward into your relationships, your community, and the world.

Ask Yourself:

- Does this action honor who I am becoming?
- Does this choice uplift others as well as myself?

This is what we mean by *ecology*: creating a life that aligns your intentions with your values and the well-being of everyone involved.

A Note on Professional Support

While these tools are deeply transformative, they're not a substitute for professional care. If you're facing challenges that feel overwhelming, we urge you to seek out the support of a licensed medical or mental health professional. You are not alone, and there is no shame in asking for help. In fact, it's one of the most courageous things you can do.

Your Results Are Up to You

Here's the beauty of this process: it works when *you* work it. The journey you take with these techniques will reflect your unique commitment to showing up, doing the inner work, and believing in your ability to change your life.

So, as you embark on this path, know this: you are worthy. You are capable. You are powerful beyond measure. Use these tools with intention. Move forward with purpose. And always, always remember you have the power to create your own results.

One more note: the Millionaire Codes are not just intellectual. To ignite their power, you must DO the step-by-step process of each code. Simply reading the book and the codes is not enough for your transformation. We've included the step-by-step process in the Part III AND for many, seeing and hearing the code steps will allow you to create even greater results. You can access the video codes and the additional worksheets and resources we mention in this book all in one place either through the URL https://millionaire.codes or via the QR Code below:

You deserve to reach and ENJOY the next level version of your life. To manifest what you desire most with EASE, WITH FUN, WITH JOY, WITH SUCCESS!

Let's DO THIS!

Time For Change

In her Forbes article *Breaking the 1.9%: How Women-Owned Businesses Reach $1 Million*, Melissa Houston shared that only 1.9% of women-owned businesses, in the USA, ever hit the $1 million mark in revenue.

1.9 percent.

This means that if you have not crossed that threshold YET, you are in the majority of coaches, experts, and entrepreneurs on the planet.

There are MANY factors that contributed to this statistic. We could spend this entire book examining the family, education, gender, cultural, societal, ancestral and genetic reasons for this, but what we really want to do is to *change* these statistics.

Part of the SHIFT we're all creating together is to focus on the SOLUTION vs the problem.

We want making a million or multiple millions per year to be the STANDARD for women business owners. More specifically, we want making your first million or millions of dollars to be the standard, the new normal, for YOU!

Our Stories

First, we want you to know that you are not alone. You don't have to suffer anymore.

We've both been in dark, invisible places, and we've discovered the path to becoming invincible.

Like so many women, we've experienced trauma and abuse in our past. But those experiences don't define us—they've shaped us into who we are today. We're sharing our stories now to inspire other women, like you, to move from feeling invisible to *invincible.*

Our stories may be difficult to hear, and we share them with deep respect for your journey. Everything we've experienced is part of our past, and each challenge gave us wisdom, strength, and insight that we now use to guide others toward their breakthrough.

If you're feeling stuck, alone, or wondering if you'll ever have the life and business you truly desire, we want you to know this: It's *possible.*

If you want it, we'll show you the way.

Today, we're living abundant, joyful lives, running businesses we love, and working with clients who are thrilled with their results. And yes, we're also in happy, loving, and fulfilling relationships.

It's possible for you too.

This book is your invitation to step into the life you've been dreaming of. It's time. Let's do this—together.

Sara's Story

In December 2017, I met with an accountant to file my taxes. His office was on the 30th floor of a building on Madison Street in the Chicago Loop. It was the kind of building that had low ceilings and beige on beige decor that made every hallway look identical. The accountant's office overlooked the brick wall of the adjacent building. A sad, browning spider plant hung over a bookshelf. The room felt airless.

After reviewing my numbers, the accountant peeled his reading glasses off his nose, peered at me over his desk and said,

"Well the good news is you won't pay much in taxes." He paused. "But my god you don't make any money."

I slunk out of the building into the cold, thin sunlight. Shame stung the rims of my eyeballs. I couldn't figure out why I couldn't make more money. Despite my best efforts, visioning, meditation, prosperity meditations, I struggled to make even $30,000 a year as an author and coach. Although my childhood was layered with trauma, what I felt worse about was that I had the privilege of a white woman with a middle-class upbringing, and an education at a top university and still couldn't create a thriving business.

Even more, perhaps like you, I KNEW I was doing the work I was here to do. I had master's certifications in life coaching, and teaching/editing books. I knew I was GOOD at writing and helping other people put their genius into words. My clients experienced personal transformation from the work as well, yet I couldn't break the invisible barrier of earning.

I did not yet know there was a very real and debilitating connection between unresolved trauma and the ability to earn money. What did my past have to do with anything, I thought. I was taking all the "right" actions in the present, wasn't I?

I'd signed up for prosperity classes and wrote affirmations on post-it notes that I stuck to the dashboard of my car and up on my bathroom mirror. I watched The Secret so many times. I read abundance books. I visualized my bank account growing and my books on the bestseller list.

But my income remained stuck. I didn't understand then that on a subconscious level, every time I tried to create a new coaching offer or introduce a product into the world, my very cells were screaming "you are broken. You aren't worth anything. You're a bad person who deserves to be punished." These were not my original words, but the words that were spoken to me in childhood, after I was assaulted by some neighborhood boys when I was six and then raped by a friend's father in third grade. They were words I told myself over and over again until they fell into a constant hum of shame and self-hatred that became as familiar as the wind. I didn't understand then that desiring something and believing we are worthy of it are two very different things. Beliefs, in the subconscious mind, like the large part of the iceberg under the water, will win every time. Just ask the Titanic.

The "earning ceiling" inside me felt like cement, not glass.

But my life was about to change. I received an email to attend a conference for heart centered entrepreneurs. Going would mean a flight from Chicago to Arizona. Two nights in a hotel. I'd never attended an entrepreneurs' conference. I felt like a fraud for calling myself a business owner when I hardly had a business. But a phrase kept humming in my brain, "you can only take others as far as you have gone." And then, "if you keep doing what you've been doing, you'll stay exactly where you are." Staying stuck in lack felt unacceptable. I wasn't contributing to my family. I was no longer willing to live out the starving artist archetype and the pay gap for women. I wanted to be a place where women and creative visionaries prospered, - where they could make millions through their genius and mission driven work.

I flew to Arizona.

The room swelled with people. Nearly 1,000 life coaches, health coaches, therapists, money and relationship coaches ranging from twenty years old to eighty pulsed through the hotel ballroom. Fuchsia spotlights strobed across the long rows of padded chairs. A DJ pumped Katy Perry's *Firework* (2010) out of speakers the size of monster trucks.

I watched women shriek as they spotted each other, like friends returning to summer camp.

I knew no one. I felt like a kid at a new school. A 40-year-old new kid. The room was electric, intimidating, exciting.

Early in the first session, the conference facilitator asked for a volunteer to come to the stage. Hundreds of hands shot into the air. I stretched my neck behind me to see who was brave enough to go on a stage to get coached in a room of that size. I shuddered, relieved it wasn't me.

A woman in the third row made her way onstage. She had bleached, cropped hair. Her sleeveless shirt revealed the kind of toned arms of someone who lifted weights multiple times per week. Michelle introduced herself and shared with the room that she was one of the top-ranking officers in her branch of the US military. The facilitator asked what she wanted to be coached on and the excitement in her body drained.

"I am grateful to serve my country," she said. "But there are 22 military suicides every day and I can't even breathe when I think about it."

The room held a collective breath while Michelle described the grief she felt, the powerlessness. "They say we're encouraged to get mental health support, but if we pursue help, we're stigmatized, so it's not an option for most people to take. Everyone's traumatized and so few of us get help."

"What do you want?" the facilitator asked.

"I feel like I have to do something," Michelle said.

I couldn't explain exactly what happened next. The coach on stage asked Michelle 5 questions from a 3-ring binder. When she'd finished answering, Michelle's shoulders tipped back, her chest expanded.

She stood up in front of her chair and palmed the microphone. Her voice boomed across the room.

"By December, I'm going to be working full time in military and veteran suicide prevention," she said. And she did.

I rushed to one of the conference team leaders at the break. "What was that?" I asked. "Those questions."

"It's called Transformational Coaching," she said. "It's based in neuro linguistic programming."

I knew I had to learn it. With a gulp, I enrolled in a $10,000 certification program. A requirement of the curriculum was to practice the NLP sequences like the one I'd just watched in Arizona. In 11 weeks, I'd made back my investment in the training. In twelve months, I had my first 6 figure year. I didn't know it at the time, but I'd just received the first download that would become the Millionaire Codes.

I'd always found making money challenging. I started babysitting when I was eleven. My first "real" job was working as a lifeguard for $4.75/hour. I did work-study at college for $5.50/hour and took a job in advertising after graduating that paid so little, my mother who was the most frugal parent I knew, dropped her head and said, "I don't know how you're going to live on this."

Finally, I reached a six-figure revenue, and it was a major breakthrough for me, but I felt an incessant calling to continue growing. I felt called to impact more people, to write new books, to move my family to a house we'd love with a large kitchen and a space for our friends to gather that felt like a sanctuary. I questioned these desires. I didn't want to be part of an American "more, more, more" paradigm. But the Universe wasn't letting this calling go. As my knees grew sore against the hardwood floor as I prayed, I heard "this is not about the money. You need to break the cycle of poverty and unworthiness off your family line. You need to contribute to the greater collective female rise." I made a promise to the leaders, coaches and experts I serve in helping them write books and make an impact speaking to also deliver a path for how THEY can make six and seven figures a year as thought leaders. We'd all spent enough time as starving artists, struggling coaches. I was NOT going to let them down.

The year I committed to going to 7 figures, I was working with a business coach who said, "as long as you can see how you'll get to your goal in a spreadsheet- you'll get there." Well, I couldn't see it. Sure I could plug in numbers and make them add up to $1,000,000 but I didn't have the confidence or mechanism to achieve those numbers through my current strategies. It was July and I was at $300,000. I didn't see any way I would reach that goal.

Then this question started to buzz in my head: what would the 7 figure CEO do? Answers and intuitive nudges began to come. Every morning, I woke up and asked this question. I wrote down whatever answer came. I started taking action on the ideas that emerged: focus on referral partners, meet with 3 every week, and guest speak at least once a month in front of a new audience. Host your own events every quarter. This was when I also began interviewing entrepreneurs who were leading 7 figure businesses and asking how they achieved this goal. I got all kinds of answers: started group coaching programs, running Facebook ads, creating courses.

One of them didn't say a word about external strategies. She said she made a list of all the limiting beliefs and feelings she had about going to a million and took that list to a specialist in subconscious/mindset work. Her answer created a buzzing sensation in my stomach. My mind flashed to Michelle on the stage that day in the hotel ballroom in Arizona. That mindset work had catapulted me to six figures. Could it help me get to seven?

I had five months and $700,000 to manifest. I was going to go all in with every possible technique that could help. I pulled out my old textbooks, began listening to hypnosis recordings at night and also engaged an expert in tapping (EFT).

Then, a colleague said I should talk to a woman named Suzanne Longstreet. "She's worked with a lot of female entrepreneurs and helped them break through into 7 figures," she said. Suzanne's cheerful face greeted me on Zoom a week later. Behind her, paintings of bursting pink flowers and paintings with swirls of purples, pink and white.

"If you focus only on what you want and do the action steps that come out of your NLP sessions, I'll work with you until you hit your goal."

I signed on that day. As I gave her my registration information, Suzanne told me people sometimes referred to her as "the Fairy Godmother".

"Like in Cinderella," she said. I could see it. Suzanne has platinum white hair, bright eyes. Her smile seemed to extend outside her body.

"From what you've told me, you're a millionaire maker," I said.

The name stuck. We started our work together in August and on December 13th, I crossed the million-dollar mark for the first time. I had achieved my goal in less than 110 days!

Suzanne's Story

I struggled with low self-worth my entire life. As a kid, I was invincible—until around eight years old. That's when the doubt set in. I started attracting mean friends who mirrored how I felt about myself. That pattern carried into adulthood, where I picked partners who tore me down instead of lifting me up.

My first marriage was the ultimate wake-up call. At first, his constant attention felt amazing. But then it started—subtle restrictions on my freedom, finances, and even the people I loved. He didn't *want* me to spend time with friends or family. He questioned everything I did. Slowly, I stopped seeing people, quit my hobbies, and even gave up buying things for myself because his outbursts weren't worth it.

And then the real abuse started—criticizing, controlling, hitting. I endured it all because I believed the lie: "It's my fault. He'll change." Spoiler alert: He didn't.

The turning point? A neighbor I didn't even know quietly told me, "If you ever need help, I'm here." That moment hit me like a brick. If *she* knew what was happening, how many others did? That shame, combined with a deep realization—I didn't want kids with him— finally snapped me out of it. I knew I had to leave.

The day I walked out, I didn't look back. It wasn't easy. The bruises healed but his voice stayed in my head, keeping me stuck. I spiraled into depression, barely hanging on.

Here's the thing: I made it. I rebuilt my life one hard, messy step at a time. And if you're in a place where you feel trapped, I want you to hear me—you can make it out, too. It's not easy, but your freedom is worth it.

After leaving my first marriage, I buried myself in work. At the office, I could drown out his voice in my head. But evenings and weekends? Those were the worst! His words played on repeat, and I felt like I couldn't escape.

I started searching for freedom from the constant noise in my head. I reached out to my family, but over time, I felt like a burden. That wasn't the answer. I tried reconnecting with old friends, but shame and distance kept me from fully opening up and sharing. That door was shut, too.

I saw a therapist. I told her I didn't want to dive into my childhood. I simply needed help surviving each day. At the end of that one session, she told me she couldn't help me. No referrals, no advice—just nothing. I left her office in tears.

I turned to church, hoping for support. When I shared my story with the leader of a divorce group, he labeled me a "D.V."—a victim of domestic violence—and told me I couldn't join. Instead, I was sent to a group for battered women. For twenty weeks, I relived my pain over and over. I left every session feeling worse, not better.

By this point, it had been 18 months since I left my husband. I pasted on a smile at work, but inside I was falling apart. My short-term memory was so bad, I had to write down everything just to get through the day. When I saw my doctor, she diagnosed me with clinical depression and suggested medication and time off work. I said no to both. Work was the only thing keeping me going, and I wasn't about to lose that.

Door after door kept closing. But deep down, I knew there had to be something—or someone—that could help me find *me* again.

During this time, I simply existed. I lived my life from moment to moment, day to day, week to week and year to year. As I was living each moment all I could focus on some days was getting through to the next day.

I had no dreams, no goals, no relationship, and no deep friendships. I was simply existing. Life was dull and grey.

I spent years living in fear, hiding from the world. I even paid to keep my name unlisted in the phone book, thinking it would protect me. Looking back, I realize how muddled my thinking was—I wasn't the only "S. Smith" in Toronto, but at the time, it felt like a lifeline.

Fear ruled my life. I stayed invisible because it felt safer that way. I believed something was fundamentally broken in me, and I spent years searching for answers outside myself. I read every self-help book, watched Oprah religiously, tried psychics, Reiki, past-life regression—you name it, I tried it. Some of it helped a little, but his voice never really left my head.

It was like being in a dark hallway with endless locked doors. No matter what I tried, I couldn't find the one that would free me. Eventually, I gave up. I stopped looking for answers and threw myself into my career.

For the next decade, I lived in the grey zone. Life was fine. I told myself it was good enough—I had a solid career and great work friends. But deep down, I knew I was just existing, not living.

Until I got fired for my behavior.

After nearly a decade of living for my job, I was blindsided: "Your services are no longer required." Fired. They couldn't even tell me exactly why. They just told me my behavior was unacceptable." I was devastated. My job was my identity, my purpose. Without it, I felt lost, like my world had imploded.

Luckily, the company offered an outplacement service, and I dove in, attending every seminar I could. A few months later, I landed a new job and made a decision: I was never going to let myself be without a backup plan again. That's when I started a coaching certification program.

Here's the ironic twist: just as I completed my first certification, I was downsized again—not for behavior this time (thankfully!) but because my role was eliminated. This time, I was ready.

Starting my coaching business was a slow, messy, agonizing process. At first, I came up with every excuse not to start. Looking back, I know I was just hiding—terrified my first husband might find me and hurt me.

I told myself I'd start after the summer. Then I met the man of my dreams (my current husband) and fell in love so starting a business felt even less urgent.

Over the next few years, I dabbled in everything but coaching—selling kitchen tools, consulting, even leading meditation groups. I avoided the very thing I wanted to do most.

After five long years, it was time to get my coaching business going. I started as a life coach but quickly realized it wasn't for me—I wasn't dealing with my own trauma and was triggered by my clients' stories. So, I pivoted to business coaching, leaning into my corporate experience in sales, HR, and organizational development.

I struggled to attract clients. Why? Because I was still invisible. So, I hired a client attraction coach. Her advice? "Go talk to 100 people." I was horrified. What if I ran into my ex? Worse, she told me to go to networking events—places full of strangers.

But the fear of failing in business was stronger than my fear of being seen. I started small, attending women-only networking events where I felt safe. Slowly, my confidence grew, and I started to attract clients.

Still, I was playing small. My coaching practice was steady but barely paying the bills. I felt stuck, constantly wondering, *What's wrong with me? Why can't I succeed like everyone else?*

Then one day, at a networking event, I met a kind therapist. Hoping for answers, I started seeing her. Around the same time, I learned about PTSD on TV and thought, *That's it! That's what's wrong with me.* But when I brought it up, she dismissed it because I hadn't been to war.

That moment confirmed something I already suspected; psychotherapy wasn't the answer for me. This door was closed. I kept searching.

The Right Door

Everything changed when I discovered Neuro Linguistic Programming (NLP). NLP is a blend of psychology, neuroscience, positive psychology, and hypnosis, and it's all about how we communicate and process the world around us. It didn't just teach me new skills—it transformed my life.

I invested in an NLP Practitioner course, and the first thing I learned was this: nothing was wrong with me. I wasn't broken. I didn't need to be "fixed." That realization alone was life changing.

The more I learned, the more I realized the power of these tools. I dove in, completing every course until I became a Designated Trainer in NLP, Hypnosis, NLP Coaching, and TimeLine™ Therapy.

During my training, I worked with a colleague also trained in NLP who specialized in PTSD. He introduced me to research about

Complex PTSD, often experienced by victims of prolonged abuse. Together, we used NLP techniques to clear it. At first, I didn't feel much different, but I surrendered to the process.

Over time, the shift was undeniable. I started showing up differently—more confident, more authentic. My self-worth skyrocketed, and so did my income. My revenue quintupled within a year. For the first time, I felt invincible.

Finding My Purpose

The tools of NLP and hypnosis didn't just change my life—they gave it back to me. The vicious voice of my first husband? Gone. The foggy, muddled thinking? Gone. I became calmer, more grounded, and deeply connected to others.

This transformation is what I call an *Invincible Mindset.* It's the result of rewiring my unconscious mind and finally stepping into my power.

I love coaching others using these same techniques, helping them shift their identity, reclaim their confidence, and achieve results they never thought possible. It's not just a career—it's my purpose.

But there was this nagging thing I couldn't ignore: my book.

For ages, I'd been trying to write my second book, but it felt impossible. I couldn't find the time, and when I did, I second-guessed every word. I kept wondering, *Am I doing this the right way? Is there a better process?* The doubt paralyzed me, and my manuscript just sat there, collecting digital dust.

Then I met Sara Connell and joined the Thought Leader Academy (TLA), and everything changed. I reconnected with my deeper *why*—why this book matters and why *I* need to be the one to share this message.

The community at TLA has been incredible. I've connected with mission-driven, inspiring people who've gone on to become award-winning and best-selling authors. Watching their success made me realize something: if it's possible for them, it's possible for me too. Being around these mission driven women made it real, and celebrating their wins alongside them has been a blast.

Since joining TLA, I've expanded my mindset, my business, and my circle of friends. And let me tell you, Sara's strategies work. In one session, she shared a workbook full of email templates. I revised one and sent it out. Within 24 hours, I had secured $40,000 in contracts—$40K from *one* email!

Sara is the real deal. She sees the potential in you before you can see it yourself, and she holds that vision until you're ready to step into it.

Looking back on my life with the clarity that comes from lessons learned, I now realize that I stayed small and invisible because I was afraid—afraid to speak up, stand up, or show up. Deep down, I lived in constant fear that my first husband would find me and hurt me.

Keeping myself invisible didn't protect me. It drained me—physically, emotionally, and spiritually. It kept me small, dim, and stuck, living a dull life. What I thought was safe was actually a cage.

Today, I'm passionate about mentoring, coaching, and sharing about NLP and hypnosis. These techniques create massive transformational shifts, fast! I love watching people step into their power, speak up, and finally take up the space they deserve.

Why This Book, Why Now?

Last year, I called Suzanne. I'd had yet another conversation with a prospective client who felt exactly as I did years before when I was stuck struggling to make any money in my business. She wanted desperately to share her "big magic" with the world, to write a book, to help more people and she wanted to earn $250K per year. "I can't get myself to write. Or make money," she said. "I feel like a failure."

Suzanne and I had begun researching the connection between earning and trauma and found there were no formal studies focused on this link. Yet, the more I coached women, continued my own inner work and dug deeper into mindset, the more I saw a relationship. In fact, I'd come to see that while for all those years I'd struggled, I thought it was inadequacy, fear, and personal weakness on my part that was responsible for my procrastination and avoidance of writing, publishing, speaking, creating, and earning, it was unresolved trauma at the root of the underearning cycle.

"You know what I wish. I wish there was a really good book - one with all the magical NLP, hypnosis, and quantum sequences we know, something anyone could pick up, instantly apply and get results, break those trauma-effect patterns and fast track them in generating abundance."

Suzanne and I examined the books on our shelves. There were good books about Neuro Linguistic Programming but in our experience, they were mostly clinical, written for practitioners, not people who'd never heard of the modality, let alone would be able to decipher the instructions and take themselves through the work.

Tony Morrison's words I'd so often quoted to my clients in Thought Leader Academy tugged at my consciousness: "if you go looking for the book you want to find but can't, it means you're the one to write it."

We put aside our other projects and began this book. Now we are so excited YOU are here and have found your way to the result of these years of study, trial on ourselves and work.

We are so excited you have found your way to THE MILLIONAIRE CODES.

Buckle up.

It's time to stop holding yourself back and start stepping into the life of abundance you're meant to live.

Let's go!

Part Two:
Welcome to the World of NLP

Suzanne's Passion for NLP

What I love about Neuro Linguistic Programming (NLP), is that it isn't some cookie-cutter approach you apply the same way every time.

It's dynamic, creative, and constantly evolving, just like baking.

Think about Red Velvet Cake. Everyone knows it for its gorgeous red colour and unique flavor, but the way it's made has changed over time. Back in the day, that red hue came from natural ingredients, beet juice or a reaction between buttermilk, vinegar, and cocoa powder. The results weren't always consistent, with shades ranging from subtle pink to deep crimson.

Fast forward to the early 20th century, and bakers started using food coloring to get that bright, bold red we all recognize today. The recipe evolved because bakers experimented and adapted.

NLP works the same way. Practitioners start with foundational techniques, the "recipe." But when they team up with clients, they adapt and tweak those techniques to meet the unique needs of the individual. It's in that collaboration, the trial and error, that breakthroughs happen.

In this book, Sara and I are sharing the techniques and approaches we've refined over the years to help you achieve real results. We've adapted NLP and blended it with other methodologies to create strategies that can increase your visibility, amplify your impact, and grow your revenue.

Just like baking the perfect Red Velvet Cake, this process is about experimenting, adapting, and finding the right ingredients to create something amazing, something that works for *you*.

Igniting Your Brain's Hidden Potential

Here's the truth. For far too long, we've been fed the idea that greatness is reserved for the "naturals", the born leaders, the gifted ones, the people who just *have it*. But here's the reality: exceptional skills, success, and the ability to rise above challenges aren't innate, they're learned.

NLP is the key to discovering those abilities already sitting inside you, waiting for you to tap into them. They are already inside of your unconscious mind, waiting for you to access them.

NLP teaches us something profound: the way you see the world, through your thoughts, emotions, and experiences, is the foundation of your reality. It's like your personal lens, and guess what?

That lens can be adjusted.

Have you ever wondered why some people light up a room while others shy away in fear? Or why someone thrives in chaos while others feel stuck? It's not because one is better than the other. It's because they've learned how to work with their mind, not against it.

Your mind is powerful, more powerful than you've been giving it credit for. If you've been feeling stuck, doubting yourself, or replaying the same limiting beliefs over and over, it's time to flip the script. With these tools, you'll see that the life you want isn't a far-off dream. It's closer than you think, it's in how you think.

This isn't just about surviving or getting by. This is about thriving. It's about crafting a life that's deeply satisfying, unapologetically yours, and wildly successful. So, are you ready to ignite your potential?

Let's go.

The Power of Your Mind

Here's the big picture: NLP is the ultimate toolkit for understanding how your brain is wired. It pulls together the best of psychology, neuroscience, positive psychology, cognitive science, and even quantum theory and hypnosis. At its core, NLP is about how you take in information from the world around you, make sense of it, and then act on it.

NLP was created by Richard Bandler and John Grinder, two brilliant minds who studied what made the best therapists, psychologists, and hypnotherapists so effective. They cracked the code on how to create real, lasting change in people's lives by rewiring how they think, talk to themselves, and behave.

What does this mean for you?

NLP is the study of excellence. It's about finding out what works, the strategies, beliefs, and behaviors of successful people, and then learning how to replicate those same results in your own life. Think of it like rewiring your brain to upgrade its operating system.

NLP doesn't just help you *understand* your brain, it gives you the tools to transform it. It's like discovering your personal superpower for better communication, stronger relationships, and unstoppable confidence.

Let's talk about how this works in real life.

Say you've got a fear of public speaking. Maybe you had a bad experience in the past, your mind has held onto that memory, and now it sends you into a panic every time you're in front of a group. NLP will help you reframe that experience, shifting your thoughts from fear to confidence. Imagine stepping onto that stage, feeling calm, collected, and ready to crush it.

NLP isn't just about boosting confidence, it's also an incredible way to process and overcome trauma. Here's the thing about trauma: it doesn't just live in your memories. It gets stored in your body and your unconscious mind laying in wait, ready to trigger anxiety or fear at the worst possible moments.

How does NLP help?

Through techniques like visualization, reframing, and anchoring, NLP gives you a way to revisit those memories and rewrite how they affect you.

That means that with the NLP techniques, you can literally recode your thinking patterns. You can work with a trained NLP practitioner to shift negative self-talk, replace fear with strength, and create new, empowering associations.

So why should you care?

Because for far too long, we've been taught that skills like confidence, resilience, and success are innate things you're born with. That's a lie. These are *learned skills.* And NLP is the key to learning them and the techniques in this book will guide you to install them so you can experience change, really fast.

NLP is all about understanding the lens through which you see the world and realizing that you can change that lens to create a whole new reality.

The Foundation of NLP

Here's a fundamental truth and one of the foundations of NLP. You are not broken. There is nothing wrong with you.

There is nothing to fix!

By the end of this journey, you'll have the insights and tools to start steering your thoughts and creating a life that isn't just good, it's extraordinary.

Are you ready to ignite your full potential?

The Big Picture

Your state, how you feel emotionally and physically, is created by two things: your internal representation (the way you process and interpret what's happening) and your physiology (what's going on in your body). That state drives your strategies, and those strategies determine your behavior.

Here's the takeaway, when you start understanding how values, beliefs, memories, and decisions are shaping your reality, you stop reacting blindly and start taking control.

You get to rewrite the script, steer your thoughts, and show up as the badass version of yourself who's ready to crush it.

The NLP Communication Model

Why Your Brain Feels Like a Hot Mess (and How to Change It)

Here's the thing, your brain is running the show, whether you like it or not. It's processing millions of bits of information every second, and most of it? You don't even notice. Why? Because your brain has one job: keep you alive. Not happy. Not successful. Just alive.

And the way it does that is by deleting, distorting, and generalizing everything that comes at you. Imagine trying to juggle 40 million ping-pong balls flying at your face. You'd freak out, right? That's what your brain deals with every single second. So, it filters out the noise and keeps what it thinks is important. The problem? Your filters were set years ago, probably before you were seven.

Here's the deal

You're walking around with outdated programming that decides what you pay attention to and how you react. These filters are based on your values, beliefs, memories, and decisions you made as a kid, like "I'm not good enough" or "I need to work harder to be loved." Yeah, that stuff is still running in the background, shaping your entire life.

Let's break it down

Deletion – Your brain is like your inbox. There's too much coming in, so it deletes 90% of it. That's why two people can experience the same thing and have completely different stories about it. Your brain keeps what it thinks is relevant, and it's usually based on your past.

Distortion – Ever blown something way out of proportion? Like when someone doesn't text back, and you're convinced they hate you? That's distortion. Your brain gives meaning to the event based on your past experience and beliefs and twists things to fit the story it already believes.

Generalization – This is when your brain says, "Oh, I've seen this before," and slaps a label on it. It's why you assume every meeting with your boss will be stressful or every workout will suck. Your brain is lazy. It generalizes to save energy.

So, what's the problem?

These filters aren't just deciding what you see; they're deciding how you feel and what you do. When your brain deletes, distorts, or generalizes information, it creates your Internal Representation, a fancy way of saying "your version of reality." That internal representation combines with your body physiology to create your state (your emotions), how you feel in the moment. And your state? That drives your behavior through the strategies that you've been running all your life.

Here's how it works

External event → Filters (deletion, distortion, generalization) → Internal representation → Emotional state → Strategies → Behavior

If you're stuck in a negative cycle, like procrastinating, avoiding difficult conversations, or playing small, it's because your filters are sabotaging you.

But here's the good news

You can change your filters. When you understand how this works, you can start rewiring your brain to focus on what matters, your goals, your dreams, and the things that make you feel unstoppable.

How?

Get Curious – The next time you're feeling off, ask yourself: "What's my brain focusing on right now?" "What is the thought that I'm having right now?" Chances are, it's deleting the good stuff and amplifying the bad.

Challenge the Story – If your brain is distorting reality ("This will never work!"), call it out. Ask: "Is that really true? Or is it just a story I've been telling myself?"

Choose a New Filter – Remember, you're in charge. You can choose to focus on what's working instead of what's not. You can decide to see challenges as opportunities instead of obstacles.

Bottom line

Your brain isn't broken, but it is a bit of a drama queen. The NLP Communication Model is like a cheat code for understanding how your mind works so you can take control. Once you learn to reset your filters, you'll change your internal state, your actions, and boom, your results.

It's time to stop letting your brain run on autopilot. You've got the power to rewrite the script.

"Your words don't define your world; your words create your world."

— Dr. Tad James

Presuppositions Of NLP

The Guiding Principles
that Change Everything

NLP is built on a set of core philosophies called presuppositions. Think of them as the framework that shapes how NLP practitioners' approach personal growth, communication, and behavior change. When you adopt them in your own life, they can completely shift how you communicate, relate to others, and approach challenges.

If you lean into these principles, you might just find yourself becoming less judgmental, more curious, and a whole lot more effective in how you navigate the world. Let's break them down.

The Map Is Not the Territory

Here's the deal, how you see the world isn't *the* world, it's just *your* version of it. This presupposition is about recognizing that everyone experiences life through their own unique filters, beliefs, and perceptions. Your map is not the same as someone else's map, and neither of them is objective reality.

When you go to a restaurant and you look at the menu, it shows you all the options that are available to eat and drink, right? Well, that's the "map", it's not what you eat. The food is what you eat. That's the "territory".

What does this mean for you? It means staying open and curious about other people's perspectives instead of assuming yours is the "right" one. Want more on this? Jump to page 116, where we dive into "Perception is Projection."

People Have All the Resources They Need

Everything you need to achieve your goals and make positive changes is already inside you. You heard that right. You might need some help accessing those resources, tools, support, or guidance, but they're there.

NLP isn't about giving you something you don't already have. It's about helping you tap into the brilliance you've been carrying all along.

There Is No Failure, Only Feedback

If you've been seeing your mistakes as failures, it's time to flip that script. This presupposition challenges you to see setbacks as opportunities to learn and grow. Instead of asking, "Why does this always happen to me?" try this: "What can I learn from this?"

In other words, if you want to go further, faster, then fail forward.

Why does this matter? Because when you shift from self-pity to curiosity, you create new neural pathways, ones that lead to growth, resilience, and better outcomes.

The Meaning of Communication Is the Response You Get

Let's get real: communication isn't about what *you* think you're saying, it's about how the other person receives it. If your message isn't landing, it's not their fault. This presupposition reminds us to take responsibility for the impact of our words.

In practice, this means being flexible. If something isn't working, tweak it. Pay attention to feedback and adjust your approach until you're making the connection you want.

Every Behavior Has a Positive Intention

This one is a bit of a brain twister and often hard for people to get at first. Even when someone's behavior seems negative, or flat-out terrible, there's a deeper, positive intention behind it. This doesn't mean excusing bad behavior, but it does mean understanding that people are usually trying to meet a need in the best way they know how.

When you recognize this, you can approach situations with compassion and curiosity, helping yourself (and others) find better ways to meet those needs.

The Mind and Body Are Interconnected

This one's simple but profound: your thoughts affect your body, and your body affects your thoughts. Ever notice how standing tall with your shoulders back makes you feel more confident? Or how anxiety can lead to a stomach ache? That's the mind-body connection in action.

NLP uses this principle to help you create change from both angles, mental and physical, because when you work with one, you're always influencing the other.

People Make the Best Choices Available to Them at the Time

This is about cutting yourself, and others, some slack. People make decisions based on what they know, believe, and have access to in the moment. It doesn't mean the choice is perfect, but it's the best they can do with what they've got.

And here's the important part: people are *not* their behaviors. Behavior can change, but the person behind it is still worthy of respect. In NLP, we separate the person from the behavior to create space for real transformation. Accept the person, change the behavior.

Putting It All Together

These principles are more than just ideas, they're tools you can use to rethink how you communicate, connect, and grow. They explain why we all experience life so differently and why arguments over "what really happened" often feel like a losing battle.

The next time you find yourself in a disagreement about the past, remember you're both working with incomplete maps of the same territory. Let go of being right and get curious about the other person's perspective.

When you embrace these presuppositions, you stop seeing the world as black-and-white and start navigating it with openness, curiosity, and compassion.

And that is how you begin to ignite the full potential of your mind and your relationships.

Prime Directives of The Unconscious Mind: Your Silent Powerhouse

Let's get one thing straight: your unconscious mind is an absolute powerhouse. It's running the show behind the scenes, managing everything from your emotions to your habits, and even how you perceive the world. The best part? Once you understand how it works, you can start working *with* it instead of feeling like it's working against you.

Here's a breakdown of the essential ways your unconscious mind has your back. Always.

1. Your Unconscious Mind Stores and Organizes Memories

Your unconscious mind is like the ultimate filing cabinet for your life. It keeps *all* your memories, both tied to time (like that embarrassing moment in high school) and timeless (those vague gut feelings that come out of nowhere). It organizes them into patterns, often using something called a Gestalt, so you can access what you need when you need it. Think of it as your brain's personal librarian, always sorting and categorizing.

2. Your Unconscious Mind Processes Your Emotions

Your unconscious mind is where all your emotions live. It doesn't just shove them into a closet and hope for the best, it stores unresolved feelings safely until you're ready to deal with them. And when you *are* ready? It helps you release them, paving the way for healing and growth.

3. Your Unconscious Mind Preserves and Runs Your Body

This one's big: your unconscious mind is in charge of your health. Your physical, emotional, mental, and spiritual health. It's like having an internal operations manager that runs everything automatically, your heartbeat, breathing, digestion, you name it. It's working with a blueprint of both your current state and your ideal health, constantly striving to keep you in balance and at your best.

4. Your Unconscious Mind Upholds Morality and Instincts

Your unconscious mind is a moral being, shaped by the values and beliefs you've picked up over your lifetime. It runs your instincts and habits, reinforcing them through repetition. This is why breaking a bad habit feels so hard, it's baked into your unconscious system. But here's the good news: once you recognize this, you can reprogram those habits to align with the life you actually *want.*

5. Your Unconscious Mind Manages Perceptions

Your unconscious mind is the gatekeeper of how you experience the world. It controls and interprets everything you see, hear, and feel, not just through your regular senses but your intuitive ones too. Every single thing you perceive is filtered through your unconscious mind and turned into a personal experience.

6. Your Unconscious Mind Works Symbolically and Takes Things Personally

Your unconscious mind is all about symbolism. It doesn't have a vast vocabulary. It loves metaphors, stories, and images, and it takes them seriously. Ever notice how a particular song or smell can instantly transport you back to a specific moment? That's your unconscious mind at work, connecting deeply personal meanings to symbols.

Here's where it gets tricky: your unconscious doesn't process negatives. If you say, "Don't think about failure," guess what it focuses on? Yep. Failure. So, keep your instructions positive, clear, and focused on what you *do* want.

7. Your Unconscious Mind Seeks Growth and Integration

At its core, your unconscious mind is always trying to help you grow. It wants you to evolve, to integrate your experiences, and to find balance. And it's smart, it operates on the principle of least effort, looking for the easiest path to success.

Why Does This Matter?

Because when you understand the Prime Directives of your unconscious mind, you unlock the ability to work with it instead of unknowingly fighting against it. Your unconscious mind isn't just keeping you alive, it's constantly supporting your well-being, growth, and success in ways you can't even see.

So, here's the takeaway: your unconscious mind is your greatest ally. It's always working in your favour, even when it feels like it's holding you back. When you learn how to harness its power, you'll feel invincible.

Meta Programs: Your Brain's Secret Operating System

Here's the thing about your brain: it's not one-size-fits-all. Your mind runs on a set of hidden patterns, what we call *Meta Programs*, and they're basically the operating system for how you think, decide, and act. And the wild part? Most of this is happening without you even realizing it.

Think of Meta Programs like filters your brain uses to make sense of the world. They're running 24/7, shaping how you see things, process information, and respond to life. They're why two people can walk into the same meeting, and one thinks, "What a great opportunity!" while the other thinks, "This is going to be a disaster."

Why does this matter?

Because if you don't know how your Meta Programs work, they're running the show, and not always in a good way. But when you *do* understand them? Game. Changer. You'll start spotting your own patterns, rewriting the ones that don't serve you, and getting out of your own way.

Here's how it works

Meta Programs are like mental settings. They're preferences that guide how you process information. Let's break down a few big ones:

1. **Toward vs. Away From**

   o Are you the type to chase goals because you're excited about what you'll gain (*Toward*)? Or do you take action because you're running from a problem (*Away From*)?

   o If you're stuck, ask yourself: "Am I focusing on what I want or what I'm trying to avoid?" Spoiler: Toward thinkers tend to feel more motivated because they're moving *toward* a dream, not just dodging nightmares.

2. **Internal vs. External Frame of Reference**

   o Do you trust your gut to make decisions (*Internal*)? Or do you need validation from others (*External*)?

   o If you're always waiting for someone else to tell you what to do, you're giving away your power. Flip the script by asking yourself, "What do *I* really want?"

3. **Options vs. Procedures**

   o Are you the kind of person who loves brainstorming and endless possibilities (*Options*)? Or do you need a clear, step-by-step plan (*Procedures*)?

   o If you're an Options thinker who never finishes anything, try narrowing your focus. And if you're all about Procedures but feel stuck, shake things up by exploring new possibilities.

4. **Big Picture vs. Detail-Oriented**

   o Do you naturally see the vision and end goal (*Big Picture*)? Or do you thrive on the nitty-gritty details (*Detail-Oriented*)?

   o The trick here is balance. If you're all Big Picture and no details, your dreams stay just that, dreams. And if you're stuck in the weeds, step back and ask, "What's the bigger purpose here?"

There's no "right" or "wrong" Meta Program. They're just preferences, like how you take your coffee. The problem is when you're stuck in one pattern that's not working for you. If you're always in "Away From" mode, for example, you're focused on what you don't want instead of creating what you do.

So, what can you do?

1. **Identify Your Patterns** – Start paying attention to how you make decisions and respond to situations. Are you motivated by fear or excitement? Do you wait for approval or trust your gut?
2. **Flex Your Style** – Your default Meta Programs aren't set in stone. If your usual approach isn't getting results, try switching it up. For example, if you're stuck in the weeds and the details, give yourself permission to dream big.
3. **Own Your Power** – The magic happens when you realize that you're actually the one in control. Your Meta Programs are tools, not rules. Use them to your advantage by aligning them with your goals.

Bottom line

Your brain is like a supercomputer, and Meta Programs are the code it runs on. It's software, not hardware and you can change the software. The more you understand these patterns, the easier it gets to rewire your brain for success. So, stop letting your programming call the shots, and start writing the rules of the game. You've got this!

Values:
Your Internal Compass

Let's talk about values, these are the deep-seated beliefs that quietly run the show in your life. Think of them as your brain's internal compass, always pointing toward what feels right or wrong, good or bad, in any given situation. They're not just preferences; they're the foundation of how you decide what matters most and how you judge right from wrong.

Here's the fun part, they change depending on the context. What's important to you at work is not the same as what drives you at home.

Here's the wild part: your values are usually buried so deep in your unconscious mind that you don't even realize they're pulling the strings. When you uncover them and align your life with what you truly value?

That's when the magic happens.

Beliefs:
The Stories You Tell Yourself

Your beliefs act as a lens through which you determine what's possible for you. They are broad generalizations and interpretations about the world that guide your every move. They're not facts (even though your brain likes to pretend they are). They're assumptions you've picked up along the way, and they're driving your behavior, all your behaviors, whether you realize it or not.

Beliefs can either work for you or against you. If you have the belief that you're not smart enough, capable enough, or whatever enough, then you'll act like it's true, even when it's not. Even though other people keep telling you it's not true, you won't believe them. When you challenge those beliefs and rewrite them to serve you? That's when you step into your power and start living the life you want.

Memories:
The Ghosts of Decisions Past

Ever wonder why you react the way you do? Here's the truth: most of your present behavior has nothing to do with what's happening right now. It's all about your past, specifically, the memories stored in your unconscious mind.

Psychologists have figured out that your reactions today are often tied to unresolved experiences from yesterday. Those memories, even the ones you barely remember, are shaping how you see the world and how you respond to it.

Decisions:
The Forks in Your Road

A lot of the decisions shaping your life today were made before you were seven years old. Yep, seven. Back then, you decided what the world meant, whether it was safe, whether you were lovable, whether you were worthy, and those decisions created the filters you use to process everything.

Before you formed beliefs, you made decisions. And those decisions? They're still influencing how you see the world and how you react to it. The good news? You can rewrite them.

Why We All Remember Things Differently

Ever get into an argument with someone about a shared memory? "You said this!" "No, I didn't!" It's maddening, right? But here's why it happens: your brain can't hold onto every detail, so it deletes, distorts, and generalizes information to make sense of it all. And guess what? Everyone else's brain does the same thing, but in their own unique way.

The next time you're in one of those arguments, let go of the need to be right (I know, it's hard). Instead, get curious. Ask, "How do they remember it?" When you stop fighting to win the memory game, you open the door to understanding.

In other words, let go of the need to be right.

Your Whole Mind

Your mind is made up of three powerful components that work together to shape your life: your conscious mind (your thoughts), your unconscious mind (your emotions), and your spiritual mind (your beliefs).

Here's how it works: your thoughts, the patterns running through your head, the words you say to yourself, and how you show up in the world all combine to create your reality.

Every single one of these parts, your conscious thinking, emotional responses, and core beliefs, works together to drive the physical results you see in your life. If you want to change your reality, you've got to start by understanding how these minds interact and influence each other.

Your Thoughts

Each thought you have creates a picture in your mind. This picture sends a message through your neurotransmitters, which bathe every cell in your body. Together, your thoughts and your physiology create your emotions.

When you create new thought patterns, you'll change your emotional responses and believe in your ability to create the results you desire in your life, your relationships, and your business.

It really can be as simple as changing your thoughts because changing your thoughts will change your reality. After all, you become what you think, feel, and believe.

Your Beliefs

Your beliefs are formed based on your life experiences, your family values, how you were treated as a child by others and what you observed. You spend the first several years of your life observing the behaviors and emotions of those around you and these combine to form your own beliefs.

It's a cycle. When you have a belief, your focus and your energy will go towards where your attention goes.

There is even a universal law in philosophy and physics that explains this phenomenon. The universal law of causality states that for every effect there is a cause and that for every cause, there is an effect. Or, as we learned in science class, for every action, there is an equal and opposite reaction.

Look around you. What results do you have that you are thrilled about? And vice versa, what results do you have that you're not happy about?

The universal law of causality states that you, and you alone, are responsible for your results. This is a challenging topic for many people to hear for the first time, because they would prefer to believe that they are not responsible for the results they have in their life or their business. They choose to create reasons and assign blame to others for why they don't have the life, the business, the body, the money they truly want.

What you think, feel, and believe you will create and become. Your thoughts and intentions influence your physical world and your results in business. In the quantum realm, just as the act of observing a particle can affect its behavior, changing your thoughts, feelings and beliefs shifts your income and impact.

Your Choice

You get to choose. You can choose to have reasons and excuses, or you can choose to have the results you want. If you choose to live your life looking for reasons outside of yourself for why you don't have what you want, you'll never have the results you desire.

Instead, choose the key to your personal power and decide to be at cause and responsible for your reality and your results. This concept can change your life and your business for the better because you'll take your power back.

Remember, every thought that you have create your emotions and your emotions drive your behaviors.

In other words, your focus determines your behavior, and your behavior determines your results. If you want to have different behaviors, then the first place to start is to change your focus and your thoughts.

This is the key to your personal power and success.

How empowering is it to know that you have created everything you have in your life right now?

Do you like all that you've created?

If you don't like everything that you have created for yourself, know that it is possible to change what you have by changing your thoughts.

This will directly change your emotions and your beliefs so that you can have what you want.

It's time to reclaim your power and create all that you want in your world.

Start by changing your thinking patterns and your emotional resilience, so that you reach your next level with ease. Transform your identity to a high performing, emotionally resilient and focused leader so that you can create the results you desire and have the income and impact you desire.

The philosophy and idea of changing your thinking to change your emotions and your beliefs to create the results you want has been in place for millennia.

Here are some quotes giving us some insights on this concept:

Buddha shared this concept during his lifetime in the 5th Century B.C. Buddha: "The mind is everything. What you think, you become."

Patanjali, author, and philosopher lived in the 2nd Century B.C. and shared "The mind is like a mirror; it reflects whatever it is focused on. Choose your thoughts wisely."

Napoleon Hill, author of "Think & Grow Rich": "The mind is the limit. As long as the mind can envision the fact that you can do something, you can do it." And "Whatever the mind can conceive and believe, it can achieve."

Neville Goddard: "You can create your own reality by changing the thoughts and beliefs that you hold." "Your beliefs become your thoughts, your thoughts become your words, your words become your actions, your actions become your habits, your habits become your values, and your values become your destiny."

Albert Einstein – "We cannot solve our problems with the same thinking we used when we created them." "Imagination is everything. It is the preview of life's coming attractions."

Dr. Wayne Dyer: "You'll see it when you believe it."

Positive thinking abounds in our culture today. More people are meditating, speaking affirmations and thinking positively. They are continually catching their negative thought patterns – or even better – catching yours - and shifting them right away.

And yet, many are still not having the outcomes and results they want.

Why?

While simply changing your thinking patterns is beneficial, sometimes, it's not enough.

Your emotions and feelings have a frequency that may be working with you or against you.

Your beliefs are deep in your unconscious mind and are running your behaviors.

Changing your thinking is good, but not everything you need. Changing your feelings (emotions) and your beliefs will create your new results because you will change how you behave.

Deep down you may be really thinking, feeling, and believing:

- It's greedy to want more money, isn't it?
- Who am I to charge more?
- What if I'm taking money from someone who really needs it?
- I can get by on just enough money.
- What will other people think or say?

When you have discovered your deep seated beliefs and shifted them so that they are no longer running the show, your actions will shift.

For some people, bringing your attention to this will clear it for you. Others who have had their beliefs tied into their unconscious mind with a deeper emotion because of an event in their past, such as trauma or bullying or abuse or deep fear, will find this more challenging to shift with just awareness.

If this seems impossible for you, I want to tell you that there is hope. Your past, your experiences, your reality has created your situation today.

Even though you've done so much to shift your mindset, I'll tell you that every single one of the millionaire entrepreneurs that I've coached has cleared out some sort of past trauma. It may have been abuse, molestation, rape, bullying or shaming. As soon as it was cleared, their path to their seven-figure business became their new reality.

When you're able to make decisions quickly, commit to your direction, focus on your outcomes, and take action easily towards your goals, you will create the income and impact you desire.

Quantum Thinking

Welcome to the Big Leagues of Your Brain

I want you to know that your brain is not just a lump of grey matter sitting in your skull, running on autopilot while you scroll through life. Nope. Your brain is the CEO of your reality, and quantum thinking is like upgrading its game from lemonade stand owner to global mogul. It's about seeing the bigger picture and realizing that *everything*, yes, everything, is connected.

In quantum physics, particles don't just sit around waiting for instructions; they're part of a system, working together in ways we're still figuring out. Your thoughts work the same way, they ripple out, influencing not just you but the whole universe.

Yeah, let that sink in. Your thoughts have swagger and a vibration.

Why does this matter?

Because what you think and believe doesn't just stay in your head. It spills into your actions, your energy, and, wait for it, your *results*. If you're stuck in the same old patterns, it's because your brain is chugging along in default mode, repeating what it already knows, instead of stepping into the limitless power of quantum thinking.

Here's a truth bomb for you: everything you've got going on right now, your business, your bank account, your relationships, is a reflection of your thoughts. Want better results? Upgrade your thoughts. It's not magic; it's science with a shot of badassery.

So, what is Quantum Thinking?

Quantum thinking is about ditching the narrow, linear view of life and embracing the fact that you're part of a giant web of possibilities. It's holistic, intuitive, and creative, because life is not a to-do list; it's an adventure.

It's the difference between saying, "I can't make seven figures because I've never done it before" and realizing, "I have everything I need to create seven figures and more, I just need to *think* like someone who already has it."

Why isn't this your default setting?

Most of us are stuck in survival mode, running outdated software from, like, caveman times. Your brain's job is to keep you alive, not to help you thrive. But newsflash: you're not dodging sabre-toothed tigers anymore. It's time to stop focusing on what's going wrong and start harnessing your quantum brain power to create what's *right.*

How do you tap into your quantum brilliance?

You start by paying attention to what you're thinking. Like, really paying attention. Every time you say, "I'm not good enough," "I can't do this," or "What if I fail?" you're basically telling the universe, "Hey, can you send more of this crap my way?"

Instead, shift the narrative. Picture yourself already living the life you want, raking in the cash, rocking your dream business, living on your terms.

Your brain doesn't know the difference between imagination and reality, so start feeding it a better story.

Quantum thinking isn't just a cute idea. It's a proven way to align your thoughts, beliefs, and actions with the results you want. Your thoughts are your GPS. If you program them to "doubt and fear," guess where you're going? Nowhere fun. But if you program them to "success and abundance," get ready to take off.

So, what are you waiting for? It's time to flip the switch, ignite your quantum thinking, and create a life that blows your mind.

The universe is ready, are you?

Your Focus

If you're like most people, you focus on the problem.

- You're stuck in a rut and not progressing your business forward
- You've tried everything and not seen the exponential growth you want or have seen others achieve
- You make sure everyone gets paid before you
- You give away a ton of your time for free
- You don't believe in yourself
- You don't charge very much
- You feel like you don't know enough to possibly charge the amount of money that you want or that others charge
- Sometimes, you feel like a fraud
- You feel anxious and doubt yourself
- You feel intimidated when you spend time with other successful entrepreneurs and leaders because you feel like they are judging you and that they are going to see that you don't actually know anything

Many people tend to overthink, ponder, and ruminate over and over on the problem. Even when you have some success, you focus on what's not going well. You may even obsess about all the presenting problems in front of you.

This is why the first question that we ask in an NLP coaching session is "Why are you here?"

It's important that you share all the presenting problems.

The process of sharing all the presenting problems is very freeing for many clients. They often don't have anyone who has taken the time or energy to listen to all the negative thoughts, worries and concerns that are spinning around in your mind.

Many clients have experienced incredible shifts by simply sharing their presenting problems. Once all the presenting problems are reviewed, you will see that there are themes to them. Often, there are simply a couple of issues that are easier to clear than dealing with all the problems.

Each of the presenting problems lead to a couple of issues and these issues are always tied to the root problem. In NLP coaching, we clear the root problem which clears the issues and the presenting problems.

In other words, when you change the root, you change the fruit.

This is why the process of NLP Coaching feels so magical. It's fast and effective.

Getting all these presenting problems out of you will help you. It's a start.

Reflection

Take time now to write out everything that is bothering you.

Why are you here?

What has happened to you in your past that you feel may be stopping you today?

The Breakdown
Before the Breakthrough

If you're in business for yourself and you've ever experienced a difficult time, you're not alone.

You may have heard the phrase, "It's always darkest before the dawn." Or "The breakdown always happens before the breakthrough."

These phrases are intended to offer comfort in difficult times. So that you know that you're not alone, others before you have experienced the dark times and the breakdowns.

In other words, don't give up during hard times because things are often hardest right before they get better.

Being aware of the signs of a breakdown will help you to embrace the breakdowns so that you can break through faster.

We've all had times in our lives when we were pushing through and then something broke down.

Being fired, getting sick, having an accident, all are breakdowns.

Some breakdowns are not as big, such as just being fatigued or frustrated, stumbling, but not falling.

They are still breakdowns, no matter how big or how small.

Here are the signs. You'll experience the emotions of boredom, tiredness, fatigue, frustration, and anger just before a breakthrough.

Here's what is really happening. These are all signs that you are about to have a breakthrough.

It's a celebration!

Pay attention to your emotions and celebrate when you experience them because you know you're about to have a breakthrough.

Your emotions are indicators of what your unconscious mind is trying to get your conscious mind to understand.

Your unconscious mind does not have language to communicate, it uses emotions, feelings, and symbols.

This is why you must pay attention to your emotions. When you experience the negative emotions of boredom, fatigue, frustration, and anger, then you'll know that something big is about to change for you.

The breakdown is happening because you need to pay attention to what your unconscious mind needs you to know. When you don't listen to your unconscious mind, you may experience an accident or an illness.

I've experienced it myself. Right before I blew up my business by sabotaging relationships with business partners and clients, I was overwhelmed with fatigue, frustration, and anger.

I just kept going and not paying attention to what my body and my emotions were screaming at me.

That's when I got snippy and short tempered with my referral partners. Then I forgot to give credit to a sponsor at an event. Then I wasn't fully present for my clients. As a result, my colleagues didn't want to do business with me anymore, the referrals stopped coming and three clients fired me in a few days.

At the time I played the victim really well and couldn't see how I had multiple warnings ahead of time. I thought that everyone was being mean to me.

I can see now, with the clarity of hindsight, that it wasn't them. It was my behavior, my actions and my thoughtlessness that caused my business to implode.

I've heard Oprah talk about this. She talks about the whisper of intuition happening first, then if that is ignored, it becomes a pebble against the window. If you ignore that, then it's a brick through the window.

I'll add that if you ignore all of these signs, then the house falls on you like in the Wizard of Oz and someone takes your shoes.

Being aware of the symptoms of a breakdown will enable you to be aware of your role in what's happening so that you can take action and breakthrough faster.

The breakdown is something to celebrate. Its purpose is to get you off the path that you're currently on. It's trying to wake you up and take away what isn't working for you so that you can discover what path you're meant to be travelling. Your role is to pay attention and ride the waves.

Change in the form of a breakthrough is happening.

Pay attention to the signs. Watch for the clues, listen to the whispers, and feel your emotions.

This is your warning to stop and assess. What's working? What's not working?

If you're seeking to level up your business, you can expect that things will change.

Up levelling and improving yourself and your business takes focus and attention.

Yes, it's always darkest before the dawn. You'll find it much easier now that you know specifically what are the indicators that you're heading towards a breakthrough.

Levels of Consciousness

Molly Jones:
From Frustration to Flourishing

Before coaching with me, Molly was stuck. She'd been working hard on her mindset, doing all the right things, or so she thought. But no matter how much effort she put in, deep down she felt like something was missing. She was frustrated, knowing she couldn't shift her thinking on her own. She sensed there were unresolved issues lingering in her subconscious, blocking her success.

During our work together, Molly made a life-changing discovery: she wasn't broken. The behaviors she called "self-sabotage" weren't failures, they were signs that her mindset needed deeper work. Through coaching, Molly realized that her past didn't control her, even the events she couldn't consciously recall.

Once those hidden blocks were cleared, everything changed.

Today, Molly knows she's not just breaking through, she's soaring. Like a phoenix, she's rising higher than ever before, not just in her business but in her relationships and her life as a whole.

The Results

Today Molly has experienced massive shifts:

In her outlook: Her views on life, business, money, and relationships have completely transformed.

In her goals: She hit her weight loss target and experiences daily wins that confirm her mindset shift.

In her business: Her revenue has more than doubled.

In her life: Due dates magically extend, unexpected opportunities arise, and money shows up in ways that feel effortless and almost magical.

She describes her new life as "inexplicable and delightful," where everything seems to work in her favour.

Molly's transformation isn't just about clearing limiting beliefs; it's about understanding the deeper framework behind human behavior and values.

What Makes This Possible? The Groundbreaking Concepts Created by Clare W. Graves.

Enter the Graves Model, which was later adapted by Don Beck & Chris Cowan and is now known as Spiral Dynamics. It is a powerful tool for understanding how our nervous system, environment, and values interact to shape our mindset and actions.

Clare W. Graves (1914–1986) was a groundbreaking psychologist who reshaped how we think about human development and behavior. His "emergent cyclical theory" of adult development became the backbone of what we now know as Spiral Dynamics, a powerful framework for understanding why we act the way we do and how we grow through life's challenges.

Graves wasn't interested in cookie-cutter explanations or rigid stages of development. Instead, he uncovered something extraordinary. He discovered that human values and behaviors evolve in response to the conditions we face. In other words, our environment.

He identified a series of value systems or "levels of existence," each one representing a unique worldview and a way of navigating life.

Here's the fun part, it's not a linear path. People move fluidly through these levels, depending on their circumstances. It's dynamic, just like life.

His work has had a massive impact, influencing everything from psychology and personal growth to how organizations understand their people.

The big idea?

Our development is driven by the interplay between who we are internally, our mindset, our wiring, and the external challenges that life throws at us.

Graves's insights are like a mirror and a map, showing us who we are and where we can go.

It's not about fixing yourself!

Remember, you are not broken.

It's about understanding the process of becoming who you're meant to be. As Mel Robbins might say: "This is about waking up to your potential and learning how to level up!"

Dr. Clare Graves developed this evolutionary human development model to explain why people think, behave, and evolve in unique ways. Understanding this model helps you as an entrepreneur to navigate your own mindset struggles and discover new pathways to success.

Change As a Journey

Imagine change as a journey, not a straight path, but one that weaves through chaos and stability.

It's like climbing a spiral staircase where each step takes you to a new level of growth. Dr. Clare W. Graves, believed that throughout life, we're constantly moving through cycles of stability (where we feel grounded) and chaos (where we grow).

The Change State Indicator

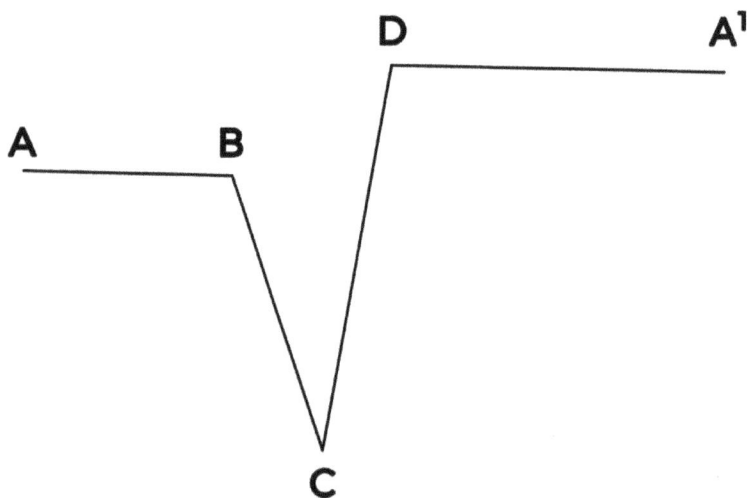

Here's how the journey unfolds:

Stage A: Feeling in Sync

At the start, everything feels manageable. Your strategies for handling life match what's happening around you. It's like riding a wave, you've got the rhythm down. Your brain, your values, and your environment are in harmony.

Stage B: The Frustration Zone

Then, things shift. What worked before stops working. Perhaps you feel frustrated, stuck, or like life's throwing puzzles at you without the right pieces. You might try tweaking things to get back to the way it was. It's like rearranging furniture in a room to make it work better without questioning if you need a new room entirely. Nostalgia might creep in, convincing you the past was perfect (even if it wasn't).

But eventually, you realize there's a bigger picture, it begins to feel like a new structure entirely. This is where deep transformation begins, guided by fresh perspectives and a willingness to evolve.

Stage C: The Sticky Spot

This stage can feel like the hardest. You're aware of the problem and even have some ideas about how to solve it, but fear and self-doubt creep in. It's like knowing the road ahead but feeling paralyzed to take the first step. Negative emotions like anger or fear might bubble up. You know what you need to do, but internal blocks hold you back. This is when the breakdown takes place. You keep trying to do things that always worked well in the past and find that nothing is working anymore.

Stage D: The Breakthrough

Finally, this is when you realize that you need to find new resources, skills or abilities and then that's when the breakthrough happens and the moment when the old ways fall away, and new strategies come into play. It's like hitting a creative spark or seeing the light at the end of the tunnel. This stage feels empowering, like you're building a new reality that aligns with your potential.

Stage A1: The New Normal

Here, you've integrated those new strategies. The world outside and the world inside you are aligned again. This new way of living feels natural, and you're thriving. But guess what? Change doesn't stop, it's a cycle, and you'll encounter new challenges that lead you to grow again.

What Does It All Mean?

For change to happen, you need:

1. Stability to start – a foundation where you feel capable of handling life.
2. A period of doubt or conflict – something shakes up your world, making you question old ways.
3. Fresh insights – a-ha moments that open new possibilities.
4. Releasing resistance – overcoming fears, negative emotions, and internal blocks.
5. Building new strategies – integrating these into your life to create lasting change.

And then, the cycle begins again. Each time, you level up, becoming a more resilient and evolved version of yourself.

This process isn't just theory, it's a map for personal transformation. Whether you're frustrated, stuck, or ready to break through, knowing these stages can help you navigate the journey with more clarity and confidence.

What Is Spiral Dynamics?

Spiral Dynamics views human development as a dynamic process where individuals and societies progress through various stages, each with distinct values and worldviews.

Note: As you read through the list below, you may be tempted to feel that you are connected more to one level or another. In fact, you have all these levels inside of you. Avoid making judgements about one level being better or worse than the others.

Here's a very simplistic snapshot of the eight values levels:

Level 1 Survival Sense: Focused on meeting basic needs like food, shelter, and safety.

Level 2 Tribal Order: Rooted in community, tradition, and a connection to ancestors. Focused on the traditional way of life.

Level 3 Egocentric: Driven by self-interest and immediate gratification. Focused on what is good for them and what they can gain.

Level 4 Absolutistic: Focused on rules, structure, and order. There is a right way and a wrong way. Most of the people in the world are at this level. This is a very corporate mentality.

Level 5 Multiplistic: Values individual achievement, innovation, and success. Seeking to be the very best they can be and make good money doing it. There are many ways, all need to be considered and assessed. This is also referred to as the entrepreneur level. You want to be the best possible you and make good money while you're at it.

Level 6 Relativistic: Emphasizes social justice, equality, and connection. Avoids conflict and believes that if there was simply more love in the world, the problems would be solved.

Level 7 Systemic: Sees the interconnectedness of systems and values big-picture thinking. Derives pleasure from simple things.

Level 8 Holistic: A deep sense of unity and the desire to create a better world.

Each stage reflects the interaction between:

Your nervous system (the biological container).

Your environment (the external factors shaping your perspective).

Your values (the beliefs driving your behavior).

How Does This Relate to Your Journey?

If you feel stuck in your business or personal life, it's likely because your values and goals are out of sync. You might be striving for something that doesn't align with what truly matters to you.

Here's what's important to remember:

You have all the levels within you. You're not defined by one stage; you can access any level depending on your situation.

When life gets tough or you're under stress, you fall back to your last fully developed stage. Think of it as old neural pathways, the mental "channels" you've used before, kicking in during challenging times.

The key to growth is understanding where you are, letting go of what's holding you back, and building new skills to move forward.

Releasing Negative Emotions to Move Forward

Every stage of development comes with its own set of limiting beliefs and negative emotions. These blocks keep you stuck. But once you release them, you gain the freedom to grow.

Here's what negative emotions and limiting beliefs show up at different levels:

Level 1 Survival Sense: Fear, anxiety, and powerlessness.

Level 2 Tribal Order: Fear of the unknown, superstition, and blind obedience. This is the way it has always been done and will always be done.

Level 3 Egocentric: Impulsiveness, selfishness, and disregard for others. Need to release shame, rage, hate, disgust and grief.

Level 4 Absolutistic: Massive guilt and self-righteousness, anxiety, fear, doubts, as well as range of repressed negative motions.

Level 5 Multiplistic: Lots of limiting decisions like fear of poverty, fear of inadequacy. Lots of anxiety, worries, doubts, inner conflicts, fear of not having enough, not making it, fear of losing it to name a few.

Level 6 Relativistic: Depression, loneliness, powerlessness. Some guilt on behalf of what we have done to the planet, hurt and a high dose of judgement.

Level 7 Systemic: Overanalyzing, getting stuck in abstraction, or lacking empathy.

Level 8 Holistic: Disconnection from practical realities or overemphasis on idealism.

The breakthrough comes when you let go of these negative emotions, blocks and limiting beliefs. It's about releasing what no longer serves you so you can evolve naturally.

The Path Forward

The key to success is about clearing the hidden blocks, understanding your values, and aligning your actions with what truly matters.

When you release the negative emotions and limiting beliefs tied to each level, you free yourself to move forward, to spiral up. This will happen in your business and in every area of your life. When that happens, the results feel magical.

The Entrepreneur's Identity Shift

The biggest identity shift for an entrepreneur is because they are taking a giant leap from Level 4 to Level 5. This transformation is monumental. Why? Because it's about breaking free from the rules and authority you once clung to and stepping into the freedom, independence, and risk-taking that true growth and entrepreneurship demands.

Here's What Level 4 Looks Like

If you're mostly operating in Level 4, you might resonate with this:

- You've been told you're the "perfect employee" because you follow the rules, stay humble, and sacrifice now for rewards later.

- You prefer a world that's black and white, clear rules, clear responsibilities, no disruptions. Ambiguity? No thank you.

- You're seeking a mentor or coach who will tell you exactly what to do, step by step. Basically, you're looking for a new boss.

- You're all about trust and rapport. If you don't trust someone fully, you'll pay them lip service, but you won't actually follow through and do the tasks you agreed you'd complete.

- Authority is sacred. You don't question it, and if it's wrong, you might sabotage quietly instead of confronting it.

- Perfection is your thing. You'll avoid taking action if it means risking a mistake.

- Schedules and stability are your comfort zone. Change and chaos? Not so much.

In Level 4, your life feels safe, predictable, and... small.

When Level 5 Thinking Starts to Open Up

Here's where things get real. Level 5 is where you begin to crave freedom. The authority you once revered starts to feel stifling. You're ready to take charge and break away, but this shift isn't smooth. It's messy, awkward, and full of internal conflict. You're tempted to just burn all the bridges and the ships and anything else that you believe is keeping you stuck.

- Suddenly, you're tired of being told what to do. You want to make your own rules, even if it feels risky.

- Friends, family, and colleagues might try to keep you "safe" or in other words "small" because your growth makes them uncomfortable. It's the classic "tall poppy syndrome" or "crabs in a bucket" phenomenon, they try to pull you back down. They might even ask you when you're going to just give up and get a real job.

- You feel torn between fitting in and standing out. You want to be different but might still pretend to be the same.

Guess what? Mistakes are not just okay, they're essential.

- Forget perfection. Stepping fully into Level 5 and being an entrepreneur is about action. Small, imperfect steps lead to progress.
- Mistakes become lessons learned, not failures. The more you embrace imperfection, the faster you'll grow.
- What you really need now isn't a boss but a coach or guide who offers encouragement, not micromanagement.

The Messy Middle: Transition Stages in Level 4

Shifting from Level 4 to Level 5 doesn't happen overnight. It's a process, and you'll feel the push and pull of both worlds.

1. If you're more in Level 4 than Level 5: You're starting to feel a spark of independence but are still heavily influenced by the authoritarian system.
2. The Tug-of-War: Your need for independence grows, but the weight of Level 4 authority keeps pulling you back.
3. Mostly Level 5: You're ready to throw caution to the wind and pursue independence, even recklessly. Be careful here, this is when you start looking for matches and accelerants to burn everything down. The structures, the rules, the authority, the bridges, the boats. Everything.
4. Level 5 Meets Level 6: Now, you're starting to notice how others intrude on your boundaries. You want to focus on yourself but still appear concerned for others.

5. The Good Girl Stage: You're trying to please everyone and be the friendly "good girl," even though deep down, you're ready to prioritize your own growth.

What Does Level 5 Look Like in Action?

When you fully step into being a Level 5 Entrepreneur, you take ownership of your life and your business. You embrace uncertainty, learn through mistakes, and build your own framework for success. You now are willing to go back and integrate the systems, processes, and structures that worked in Level 4 and integrate them as lessons learned so you can scale up and level up.

The shift from Level 4 to Level 5 is a quantum leap into your next evolution. This is when your identity shifts. This is where you stop playing small and start creating the life and business you're truly meant for.

Here Be Dragons

Remember a time when you started something new. It could be a new business, a new project, or launching a new product or service.

You may have felt trepidation; a hammering heart, sweaty palms, spinning thoughts.

You may have said mean things to yourself, like "this'll never work," or "you'll never amount to anything." You may have even visualized yourself failing horribly. Worse, you may have imagined the rotten things that other people may say about you.

Guess what? You're completely normal. It's a human trait. You've come by it naturally.

In ancient times, the cartographers who created maps would write "Here Be Dragons" in the unexplored areas.

> "Here be dragons means dangerous or unexplored territories, in imitation of a medieval practice of putting illustrations of dragons, sea-monsters and other mythological creatures on uncharted areas of maps.", Wikipedia

These thoughts, fears, and trepidations are simply the dragons of uncharted territory. It's the fear of the unknown that you're experiencing which is a completely normal and healthy concern.

It's your Amygdala. It is still assessing threats and determining if you need to freeze or take flight or fight.

You might be sitting there thinking, *"Wait a second. If my unconscious mind is supposed to keep me safe, why does it also keep me from doing things that could make me successful—like putting myself out there, building my business, or asking for the sale?"* It's a fair question! I mean, wouldn't the part of you that's supposed to protect you also want you to have all the abundance, freedom, and success you dream of?

Of course it does. But here's the truth, your unconscious mind is trying to do both: keep you safe *and* help you grow. The problem? It has an overzealous part named the Amygdala. This little part of your brain is like the alarm bell of your emotions. It's there to keep you from getting eaten by lions (okay, maybe not lions anymore, but you get the point). When you step out of your comfort zone, your Amygdala freaks out. It's like, *"Danger! Red alert! Unknown territory ahead!"* That's all it is. It's your brain's fire alarm going off when it senses anything new.

Here's the secret sauce: *you* are in control. When you start taking action, even baby steps, the alarm starts to quiet down. Isn't that cool?

Each step you take, each move you make toward your goals, sends a powerful message to your brain: *"Hey, this isn't dangerous. There are no dragons here. It's actually kind of amazing!"*

And suddenly, that scary voice in your head? It starts losing its power. The negative thoughts fade away, and you know what replaces them? The thrill of success, the joy of accomplishment, and the realization that *you're doing it.* So yes, your unconscious mind wants you to be successful, but it's up to *you* to remind it that stepping into the unknown isn't dangerous—it's where the magic happens.

As you move towards your goals, you will continue to prove to your unconscious mind that you're safe and protected while moving towards greater abundance and success.

Now, get out there and show that Amygdala who's boss!

If these feelings don't disappear and you're still stuck and not moving forward, then it may be for a bigger reason. It may be because your unconscious mind is running a program so deep, you're not aware of it.

Here's What's Been Happening In Your Unconscious Mind

Your unconscious mind and your thoughts are so incredibly powerful. Your unconscious mind is continually working on your behalf by sending up information in the form of emotions, or memories from your past, to get your attention for your highest and best good.

For years, you may have squashed down your fears and your negative thoughts and your negative emotions. Perhaps, you have switched your thoughts from the negative patterns to something positive. When something negative does manage to pop up, are you mean, demeaning, disparaging and judgmental about yourself for having these negative thoughts in the first place?

Simply pushing these thoughts and feelings aside will not make them go away or resolve them. They will just get buried deeper in your unconscious mind and will run when they are triggered.

Those negative emotions, fears, thoughts, and behaviors are running on a loop in your unconscious mind. They are background noise that you may not be able to hear or even know are there. They are so far embedded in your unconscious mind, that they have you running on autopilot.

You don't know that the program is running until you're triggered by someone or something happening and then you react emotionally. You may cringe and run away, or you may get mad and say things you don't mean. In the moment, this seems the best way to behave. It's almost as if a different part inside of you has engaged and taken over control of your reactions.

It's only afterward that you wonder what got into you.

If you've been refusing to listen to the negative thoughts that are coming up from your unconscious mind as many of us have been told to do, then it's time for you to start paying attention to those thoughts.

Paying attention to that voice inside of you will be instrumental in discovering what may be stopping you from greater success.

Remember, Your Unconscious Mind Is Programmed to Protect You.

Your unconscious mind is hard-wired to seek out and find threats to your survival. The human species has evolved from a time when we lived to kill for our food or be killed. We had to hone our survival instincts to quickly assess each situation and determine if there was an imminent threat and we needed to either take flight or fight.

Since you're here today, this proves that your ancestors developed the ability to assess threats and take the right action for survival over others.

How Your Mind Is Wired

Let's start with this: your mind is an absolute powerhouse when it comes to processing information. Every single second, it's bombarded with over 40 million bits of data, everything you see, hear, feel, smell, and taste. Again, that's like having millions of ping-pong balls flying at you all at once.

Your brain isn't designed to process all of that. If it tried, it would completely shut down. Instead, it uses filters, your experiences, values, beliefs, morals, and attitudes, to sort through the chaos. Those filters decide what gets deleted, distorted, or generalized to make things manageable. It's a brilliant system, but it's also why your reality looks totally different from someone else's.

Your Brain Is Holographic

Here's a fun thought experiment: if you cut an apple in half, you get two halves. But if you cut a hologram of an apple in half, each piece still contains the entire apple, just with less detail. Your brain works like that hologram.

Scientists believe that your thoughts, memories, and experiences aren't stored in one specific spot. They're spread out across your brain, and every piece contains the whole. That's why your memories of events, especially emotionally charged ones, aren't just factual. They're influenced by your beliefs, emotions, and the filters running in your mind.

You don't just store information sequentially (over time). You also store it outside of time. For example, you might recall a specific sequence of events from yesterday, but general knowledge or emotional triggers? Those aren't tied to a timeline, they're wired into your unconscious mind.

Let's Illustrate:
The Fear of Public Speaking

Here's a story: Sadie is a little girl who loves sharing stories with her family. One day, she starts telling a story, and halfway through, she hears laughter. She immediately feels a wave of shame and humiliation. In that moment, her brain wires those emotions to the act of speaking up.

Here's what actually happened: the laughter was coming from the TV playing in the background. But Sadie's unconscious mind didn't know that. It decided that speaking up = feeling horrible, and to protect her from ever feeling that way again, it created a program to shut her down whenever she tried to speak up.

Flash forward to adulthood. Sadie has big dreams, but every time she wants to present, share her ideas, or take the stage to grow her business, fear and shame take over. Her unconscious mind is running the show, scanning for any tiny sign, body language, facial expressions, a slightly negative tone of voice, that proves it's right to protect her by holding her back. Her reticular activating system (RAS) is always on guard and searching for these signs. It is protecting Sadie from having a similar experience.

Now imagine if Sadie could revisit that moment as an adult. She'd realize the laughter wasn't about her at all. It was the TV. That single shift in understanding could completely rewrite the story her unconscious mind has been playing for years. Her life, career, and business would be transformed.

How Does This Apply to You?

If you've ever experienced trauma, negative events, or even just repeated rejection, your unconscious mind has likely written programs to protect you. That's its job. It doesn't want you to feel pain, so it runs strategies to keep you safe.

But here's the thing: those strategies, while protective, can keep you stuck. They don't just disappear because you want them to. Most of the time, the programs are so deep in your unconscious mind that you can't reach them with conscious effort alone.

Why You Can't Just
"Think Your Way Out of It"

Dr. Bruce Lipton, in his book The Biology of Belief, explains this perfectly. He compares trying to change your unconscious programming without the right tools to yelling at a TV show you don't like. You can shout, "Don't go in there!" or "Just get in the car!" all you want, but it's not going to change the prerecorded episode.

The same goes for your unconscious mind. You can't outthink it. You need proven tools like NLP or hypnosis to get in there and rewrite the program.

What Happens
When You Relive Trauma

Here's why just talking about your trauma over and over doesn't always help: your unconscious mind doesn't know the difference between past and present, what's real or what you imagine. When you relive a traumatic memory in vivid detail, your unconscious thinks it's happening right now.

If you're retelling the story with present-tense language, you're essentially re-installing the same fear, pain, and negative patterns into your mind. That's why it can feel worse after sharing your story, not better.

How to Move Forward

There is good news! Your unconscious mind can be rewired with the right approach. NLP and hypnosis are incredibly effective tools for clearing old traumas and rewiring those deep, automatic programs.

If you've tried everything else and still feel stuck, this might be the missing piece. Your unconscious mind isn't working against you, it's doing its best to protect you. With the right guidance, you can teach it to work for you instead, helping you move out of fear and into action.

The Link Between Trauma and Earning

Let's talk about something I've seen again and again with my clients. Past trauma holding them back in ways they didn't even realize. When we work together to clear that trauma, the results are incredible, greater income, more fulfilling relationships, skyrocketing self-worth, and a whole new sense of freedom.

Here's the truth: trauma isn't just something that happens in your past. It's something your mind and body carry with you, influencing how you think, feel, and behave every single day.

What Is Trauma?

Trauma, at its core, is your emotional response to a distressing event. The American Psychological Association describes it as "an emotional response to a terrible event like an accident, rape, or natural disaster." But trauma isn't always about those big, life-threatening moments.

According to the Centre for Addiction and Mental Health (2022), trauma can also be the "challenging emotional consequences" of events like abuse, neglect, a breakup, or even job loss. It can hit hard and fast, or it can build up over time. Either way, trauma can leave a lasting imprint on your mind and body.

Small "t" vs. Big "T" Trauma

You've probably heard people describe trauma as either "small t" or "big T." Let's break it down:

Big T Trauma: These are the major, life-altering events that can lead to PTSD or serious mental health challenges. Think natural disasters, assault, severe abuse, or witnessing a violent crime. It's the kind of trauma most people immediately recognize because it's intense and overwhelming.

Small t Trauma: These are the smaller, cumulative events that might not seem like a big deal on their own but add up over time, things like bullying, job stress, a breakup, or financial struggles. While they're less intense, their impact can be just as significant because of their buildup.

Here's the thing: whether it's a big T or small t trauma, what matters most isn't the event itself. It's the meaning you give to that event.

Be Kind to Yourself

Too often, I hear clients downplay their experiences. "It wasn't that big of a deal," they'll say, or "I should be over this by now." But here's the truth: what happened to you matters. Whether it's big T or small t trauma, if it's affecting your ability to achieve your goals or live the life you want, it's real, and it's worth addressing.

Stop comparing your experiences to anyone else's. Trauma isn't a competition. You are unique, and so is your response to what happened to you.

The Meaning You Give to Events

The impact of trauma isn't about the event itself, it's about the meaning you assign to it. As Tony Robbins says, "Nothing in life has meaning except the meaning you give it."

Let me share a story about a client. She remembered sitting on the couch as a child, watching TV with her sister while their neighbour, a young man babysitting them, engaged in inappropriate behavior.

My client couldn't stop thinking about it. Decades later, she still carried feelings of inferiority, shame, and low self-worth.

Her sister? She didn't even remember the event. She had a thriving career, a loving relationship, and no lasting impact from that day.

Why the difference? Each sister gave the event a different meaning. One internalized it as something shameful that shaped her self-perception. The other unconsciously dismissed it as irrelevant and moved on.

Why Trauma Affects Everyone Differently

This brings us to a key principle of NLP: your unconscious mind's main job is protection.

One sister's unconscious mind protected her by erasing the memory. The other sister's unconscious mind protected her by keeping it front and center to guard against future harm.

Neither response is "right" or "wrong." It's just how their unconscious minds chose to protect them.

The problem comes when the meaning we've given to an event keeps us stuck. That meaning, those emotions, beliefs, and behaviors, gets wired into our neurology. As Donald Hebb famously said, "Cells that fire together, wire together."

If those patterns can be wired in, they can also be rewired. And that's where the magic happens.

Trauma and Your Unconscious Mind

Here's why you can't just "get over it": your unconscious mind doesn't know the difference between past and present. When you relive a traumatic memory, your body and mind respond as if it's happening right now.

This is why talking about trauma over and over, without the right techniques, can often make things worse. Your unconscious mind re-installs the same fear, shame, or pain every time you replay the story in vivid detail.

Again, it's like yelling at the TV screen. You can scream all you want, but it's not going to change the story.

Recoding Trauma for Growth

Here's the good news: trauma doesn't have to define you. The same way your unconscious mind wired those old beliefs and emotions, it can unlearn them.

You read that right. It can be unlearned as quickly as the trauma happened. Not years or decades.

NLP and hypnosis are incredibly effective tools for clearing trauma and rewriting those deep programs that hold you back.

If you've experienced trauma, big or small, and find yourself stuck, unable to grow, or afraid to step out of your comfort zone, it's time to stop fighting your unconscious mind and start to rewire it.

The meaning you've given to your experiences has shaped your life. But here's the truth: you have the power to change that meaning and create a new story.

Vicarious Trauma
or Compassion Fatigue

I met Jessica at a conference several years ago. She is a beautiful young woman in a successful professional career. When she approached me at the conference, she whispered that she had suffered trauma and was struggling in her life.

She had some very big goals for her life. Yet, she found that the harder she worked, she couldn't quite get to do the things she wanted to do. She was not in a relationship, and she dearly wanted to be in a loving relationship. She was working in a corporate role, and not being the creative entrepreneur and thought leader she aspired to be. She was incredibly frustrated and kept investing in courses and EMDR (eye movement desensitization and reprocessing) therapy and was still unable to fully clear the mindset blocks that were in her way.

As we began to work together, we soon discovered that what was stopping her was the trauma her sister had experienced because of domestic violence. My client was demonstrating all the symptoms of vicarious trauma. The real problem, if you can call it that, was that she is a loving and compassionate sister who was dismayed by the trauma her sister had experienced repeatedly.

After the NLP coaching, she transformed the way she thinks. Her life is different now because her mindset is different. She is no longer forcing herself to do things. Her focus is now much for positive. She is much more excited for her future.

Best of all she started to see someone and was excited about feeling all her feelings and being vulnerable in her new relationship. About a year after our coaching finished, she shared that she is still in a relationship with the same person and that "he is not the man of her dreams, he's better."

Today, she is happy and fulfilled in her current chapter of life, personally and professionally.

She shared that while the different forms of therapy she enrolled in over various years, including talk and EMDR, contributed to her healing, the NLP ultimately seemed to offer clarity and peace in her body and mind.

Jessica's story is proof that trauma doesn't have to happen *to you* for it to affect you. You can feel the weight of trauma just by being deeply connected to someone who's been through it. Vicarious trauma is more common than you might think.

I worked with two incredible clients who experienced this firsthand. Both had siblings who went through traumatic events, and because they were so compassionate and empathic, my clients unknowingly *took on* the emotional pain themselves. They weren't the ones who experienced the trauma, but they carried it as if they had.

Here's the amazing part: once we uncovered what was happening and worked through it, everything changed. Today, they're living lighter, happier lives. They've let go of what wasn't theirs to carry and stepped into a whole new sense of joy and freedom.

Trauma doesn't have to define you—especially when it's not even yours to hold. There's always a way forward.

The Root of Change Starts In Your Mind

Here's a truth that's hard to ignore: the root of all healing begins in your mind.

Epigenetics, the study of how behaviors and environment can change the way your genes work, has shown us this in groundbreaking ways.

As Dr. Deepak Chopra puts it, "The immune system is constantly eavesdropping on the internal dialogue." In other words, your thoughts and beliefs don't just live in your head, they ripple out into your entire body, shaping your health, resilience, and ability to heal.

You're not just dealing with the traumas you've experienced personally. Your unconscious mind might also be carrying the weight of traumas passed down through your family line.

This is called intergenerational trauma, and it's not just a theory, it's backed by science. Researchers have found that trauma experienced by one generation can create epigenetic changes, literal shifts in how genes are expressed, that are passed down to the next.

Think about that for a second: you could be carrying the echoes of pain, fear, or survival strategies from events you've never even experienced firsthand.

But wait, here's the good news: just like your mind can carry those patterns forward, it also has the power to break them. Changing what's been passed down isn't just possible, it's transformational.

Trauma Symptoms

What's Keeping You Stuck

Trauma doesn't just live in your past, it shows up in your life, your business, and your relationships in ways you might not even realize. Here are some of the most common trauma symptoms I've seen in clients before they do the work to clear them:

Isolation

- Avoiding going outside or being in public.
- Pulling back socially and staying guarded with friends and family.
- Limiting contact with people, clients, or opportunities.

Invisibility

- Avoiding social media or skipping videos altogether.
- Being hyper-critical of how you look in photos or sound on videos.
- Judging yourself harshly and choosing to stay in the background.

Insecurity

1. Staying quiet, doubting that your perspective has value.
2. Avoiding speaking events or networking opportunities.
3. Not sharing your services, ideas, or products with confidence.
4. Struggling to make decisions or hesitating to invest in yourself.

Low Income

- Paying others but not paying yourself.
- Undervaluing your services and not charging enough.
- Feeling ashamed for wanting to double or triple your revenue.

Here's the connection:

Isolation + Invisibility + Insecurity = Your Income Level

These behaviors, rooted in trauma, are like an invisible force holding you back.

Here's the powerful part: once you clear them, that force shatters.

When you do the work to clear these patterns, the results are nothing short of transformational. Some of the results clients have shared:

- Deeper, more fulfilling relationships, both personally and professionally.
- Calmer, positive and confident mindset that allows them to show up fully.
- Charge their worth without hesitation, growing their income and their impact.

The shifts are life changing. For some, it's achieving greater business success. For others, it's leaving relationships that no longer serve them or stepping into new opportunities they've always dreamed of.

Clearing these blocks is about stepping into the person you've always known you could be. It's about experiencing a deep and profound identity shift. The freedom, confidence, and joy that come on the other side of the work? That's where you soar.

Dr. Ingryd Lorenzana: From Stuck to Soaring

Before working with me, Ingryd felt stuck. She had been pouring her heart into personal growth, emotionally, physically, and spiritually, and doing everything she could to improve herself and her business. But despite all her effort, she wasn't seeing the results she hoped for.

She kept asking herself:

- "What else is out there?"
- "Why am I stuck?"
- "Why isn't my hard work paying off?"
- "What is going on?"

She was aware of her challenges, but what she didn't realize was that there were deeper, hidden blocks holding her back. During our coaching, those blind spots came to light, and the discoveries were truly transformative.

Ingryd had been feeling defeated, wondering if all her work was ever going to pay off. Her big aha moment came when she uncovered the things she didn't even know were blocking her, negative emotions, limiting beliefs, and even ancestral guilt she didn't realize she was carrying.

When we released those blocks, everything shifted. She let go of guilt and other emotions that had been weighing her down for years. As a result, all the work she had done before, therapy, self-improvement, and personal development, finally started to click in ways it never had before.

The Results? Tremendous Growth and Confidence

Since our work together, Ingryd's business has grown.

- Her business grew by 30% in the first quarter after our coaching.

- She moved into a new space and is building momentum like never before.

- Most importantly, she feels invigorated and confident, knowing she's no longer carrying the emotional baggage that was holding her back.

Today, she's stepping fully into her potential, confident that all the effort she's put in will get her to her big goals. The transformation she's experienced has not only helped her business blossom but also renewed her energy, mindset, and belief in what's possible.

Ingryd's story demonstrates that when you clear what's blocking you, emotionally and unconsciously, you open the door to results beyond what you thought was possible.

Believe In Your Potential

"Our deepest fear is not that we are inadequate. Our deepest fear is that we are powerful beyond measure. It is our light, not our darkness that most frightens us. We ask ourselves, 'Who am I to be brilliant, gorgeous, talented, fabulous?' Actually, who are you not to be? You are a child of God. Your playing small does not serve the world. There is nothing enlightened about shrinking so that other people won't feel insecure around you. We are all meant to shine, as children do. We were born to make manifest the glory of God that is within us. It's not just in some of us; it's in everyone. And as we let our own light shine, we unconsciously give other people permission to do the same. As we are liberated from our own fear, our presence automatically liberates others."

— Marianne Williamson

You can choose to remain where you are, or you can make the choice to change.

Here's what I believe in the deepest part of my being; if you have the dream and desire to be a millionaire business owner you can achieve all that you want, dream, and believe.

If you have the desire and the will to be making an impact and a difference, then you can.

If you can conceive the idea, you can achieve it. It's time for you to ignite your potential now.

Too often, I watch many entrepreneurs, especially female entrepreneurs, stop themselves. I've watched them shrink and not share their success because they don't want others to feel small or less than.

So why do so many people do it?

Because, deep, deep, deep down they believe that it is keeping them safe. It's a form of protection.

So, what's the answer?

Start by paying attention to the thoughts that you have in every moment. It's not easy to do at first because you've spent years pushing them down, tuning them out or talking over them with positive affirmations.

Be mindful of how you describe yourself, your life, your relationships, and your business to other people. Listen to the thoughts you have about yourself that may be holding you back in your business.

It's time to tune in and listen.

Your thoughts are *everything*. They're like breadcrumbs leading you to the unconscious beliefs that are running the show. If you want to crack the code on what's holding you back, start paying attention to what's rattling around in your head.

Writing your thoughts down isn't just journaling—it's the roadmap to your success. It's how you uncover what's working for you and what's sabotaging you. Want proof? Julia Cameron shared this in *The Artist's Way* with her game-changing practice called Morning Pages. It's simple, transformative, and wildly effective.

Every morning, grab a notebook, start writing, and let your thoughts pour onto the page. The best time is first thing in the morning before your brain fully wakes up. Simply write. Get your thoughts down. They will show you the way forward. This isn't just busywork; it's the key to igniting your potential.

Here are some reflective questions to guide you to connect more deeply with your thought patterns:

1. What do you really want?
2. What ignites a strong emotion (either positive or negative) inside of you when you hear or see someone else doing it?
3. What do you find yourself talking about doing over and over?
4. What specific actions are you taking now that are moving you towards your goals?
5. Do people in your life keep reflecting something back to you about yourself? What are they telling you?

Here are some of the limiting beliefs that clients have shared with me. Do you have any of these thoughts?

- Who am I to have a successful business?
- What do I know that will make a difference in the world?
- I don't believe I can do this
- I don't want to charge that much for my services
- I feel like I am just existing from day to day
- I have no idea how to get out of where I am today
- I don't have a clear vision of what I want
- If I just keep making sacrifices, life will get better
- I fear conflict and don't stand up for myself
- I have tolerated being bullied or abused
- It's just a matter of time before I am abandoned or rejected
- I feel like a fraud
- I feel like a failure
- I need to stay humble, so I mustn't brag

- I need to deflect compliments
- I must be nice
- I don't get angry
- Strong women don't ask for help
- Saying no will hurt their feelings

Start by writing out some of the ones above if they resonate with you and keep adding as you progress through this book.

What thoughts do you have about yourself that are holding you back from success?

Begin With Your Thoughts

Every single thought you have, especially the ones packed with emotion, programs your unconscious mind. Those thoughts create your beliefs. Your beliefs drive every single action you take, and your actions create your results.

If you're not getting the results or the success you want, it's time to take a hard look at your thoughts. The difference between crushing your goals and falling short? It's in the infinite potential of your thinking.

Now, here's the truth, it's completely normal to have doubts. We all do. You wonder if you're doing enough, doing the right things, or if you're even cut out for this. Those negative thoughts? They're not random. They're coming straight from your unconscious mind, and they have one job. That job is to keep you safe.

Your unconscious mind doesn't care about growth or success; it's all about survival. When you try something new or step outside your comfort zone, it throws fear at you—memories, emotions, even full-blown panic. Why? Because to your unconscious mind, different equals dangerous.

Here's the thing, your unconscious mind isn't your enemy. It's just doing its job. It thinks it's helping you by keeping things exactly as they are. So don't blame it. Instead, recognize it. Thank it for trying to keep you safe, and then tell it, "I've got this."

Because here's the truth: you *do* have this. It's time to reprogram those thoughts and take control of your actions.

Start by paying attention to what you're saying to yourself and about yourself.

Listen to how you describe your thoughts and beliefs to another person. Pay attention to what you're saying to yourself over and over. Pay attention to what you say about yourself when you're speaking with others. These are the clues to what is playing repeatedly in your unconscious mind.

Stop using present tense language to think about and describe what happened to you in the past. Use your language to remind yourself that the traumatic events happened in the past and keep them in the past.

Starting right now, I want you to get real about the thought patterns that aren't serving you. It's time to uncover the significant emotional events—what we call *SEEs*—from your past. These are the moments that shaped you, whether you realized it or not.

Here's how: Write out your life story. Don't overthink it—just start. Pay extra attention to the events that triggered a strong emotional reaction. It doesn't matter if the emotion was positive or negative. What matters is that the event was *significant.*

For each event, ask yourself: *What emotions were present?* Write them all down. Be honest. Be thorough.

Here's an important note: many of these patterns began before you were even 7 years old. That's often when the behaviors that are holding you back today first took root. If you can, try to recall as many of those early significant emotional events as possible.

And listen, if you experienced major trauma in those early years, this might feel tough—and that's okay. Your mind might be protecting you by blocking out certain memories. Be kind and gentle with yourself. There's no need to push. Just write down what you can.

Once you've got your list, take a step back. Review the emotions and feelings that came up. Here's why this matters: *"How you do anything is how you do everything."* These patterns, emotions, and beliefs have been running on autopilot, shaping how you show up in the world.

This process is about shining a light on them. By simply identifying these SEEs and the emotions they stirred, you'll begin to unravel how your brain has been programmed over the years. These patterns and stories that feel so permanent? They're just part of your past. And here's the exciting part: you're about to use the Millionaire Codes to rewire your brain and rewrite those patterns for success so that you RISE.

Goals & Outcomes

Let me be real with you—there's a lot of chatter out there about *not* setting goals, and honestly, it's dangerous. Sure, you've probably set goals before and fallen short. We've all been there. But here's the deal, some people never set goals at all. Like, not even one. And that? That's a recipe for staying stuck.

If you don't know what you want, you're not living intentionally. You're floating through life, waiting for someone else to tell you what to do next or—worse—living for other people's expectations. That's no way to live!

Here's the truth: your intention is EVERYTHING. Goals aren't just about hitting a target. They're about getting clear on what you truly want—your deepest desires, needs, and dreams—and aligning your energy to move toward them. When you set a goal with real intention, you give yourself direction and purpose.

Without goals, life will toss you around like a raft in a white-water river with no paddle. You might get lucky and land somewhere great, but chances are, you'll end up stuck or drifting aimlessly.

So, ask yourself: What do you *really* want? What's the life you're dreaming of but haven't admitted to yourself yet?

Write it down. Set the goal. Focus on it.

When you know where you're going, you can get there—and trust me, the journey will be worth it

Here's an example of what you're really doing when you don't set intentional goals.

Imagine sitting at a table in your favourite restaurant and when the server approaches you to take your order you can't make up your mind as to what you want to eat. So, you say to the server "oh, just bring me whatever you think I want to eat."

How do you think that's going to go?

What will you end up eating? Will you enjoy it? Will you send it back? Will you eat it and lament about how once again you didn't get what you really want?

Now, compare this to your business. Are you clear in your desires? Are your intentions specific? Here's a hint, if you don't have the results you want, including the money, abundance, clients, and impact you desire, you're not being specific and intentional.

Being intentional is crucial for your success. In the realm of NLP, one of the most emphasized phrases is "Say it the way you want it." Your intention plays a pivotal role in your success, and expressing your desires positively programs you for achievement.

Research from the 1970s revealed that a positively stated goal is more achievable than a negatively stated one. Your focus drives your behavior, and your behavior, in turn, creates your results.

Energy follows attention, so it's essential to be mindful of what you're focusing on in every moment. Your results are simply feedback on where your attention is directed. So, pay attention to what you're focusing on at every moment. You are programming your unconscious mind with every single thought.

Here's the NLP process to ask yourself questions about your goals and help you to be more specific and intentional.

Keys To an Achievable Outcome

1. Stated in the positive.

"What specifically do you want?" Make sure that the outcome is stated positively.

2. Specify your present situation.

"Where are you now?" Be very specific and clear about what you have now and describe the emotions you're feeling as well.

3. Specify outcome.

"What will you see when you have it?"

"What will you hear when you have it?"

"What will you feel when you have it?"

(Make sure that your answers are compelling, specific, and positive.)

4. Specify evidence procedure.

"How will you know when you have it?" Be specific. If your first thought is about a feeling or emotion, go deeper to be more specific. We haven't figured out yet how to measure confidence or happiness. Your unconscious mind needs to focus on a specific, tangible measure. Evidence procedure could be an amount of money in your bank account, the number of clients you would love to work with, a stage you want to speak on, number of followers. These are specific outcomes.

5. Is it congruently desirable?

"What will this outcome get for you or allow you to do?"

6. Is it self-initiated and self-maintained?

"Is it only for you?" (This trips up a lot of people. They believe that the best way to achieve the goal is to make sure that it's for everyone else and not themselves. While that is very noble of you, your unconscious mind won't get on board and make it happen for you. So, you must convince yourself that it is for you first, then others.)

7. Is it appropriately contextualized?

"Where do you want it?"

"When do you want it?" (Make it a specific date. Include the day, month, and year. Otherwise, your unconscious mind won't get to work on it for you as it will simply put it off to an uncertain date in the future.)

"How do you want it?"

"With whom do you want it?"

8. What resources are needed?

"What do you have now, and what do you need to get your outcome?"

"Have you ever had or done this before?"

"Do you know anyone who has?"

"Can you act as if you have it now?"

9. Is it ecological (is it good for you, your family, your business, your clients, your community, the planet)?

"For what purpose do you want this?"

"What will you gain or lose if you have it?"

Finally, create a picture of yourself having all that you want as if it's already taken place and imagine being able to insert it into your future. Make sure that you can see yourself in the picture. This will program your unconscious mind to go for it.

Here's the secret for attracting what you want faster. Engage all your senses, sight, sound, feeling, smell and taste. The more detailed and specific the picture in your mind of what you want is, the easier it is for your unconscious to grasp it and start to attract it to you. When you see yourself in the picture having your goals met and your dreams attained, your unconscious mind will make it happen for you. If you don't see yourself in the picture, your unconscious mind will believe you already have it, so it will feel hard. You'll feel like you're fighting yourself every step of the way, because you are. So, engage your whole mind by seeing yourself in the picture and make it easier for yourself to reach your dream goals and desires.

The more clarity you have of what you want, the easier it is for you to tap into the quantum realm.

Your conscious mind is the goal setter, and your unconscious mind is the goal getter.

When I'm doing a workshop, we sing this. So imagine saying this over and over again in a singing voice.

My conscious mind is the goal setter, and my unconscious mind is the goal getter.

My conscious mind is the goal setter, and my unconscious mind is the goal getter.

My conscious mind is the goal setter, and my unconscious mind is the goal getter.

So, set an intentional goal and program your unconscious mind to go get it for you.

Yes, it's that simple.

Perception Is Projection

> "The information, which is most unconscious in us, we, by need, must project onto someone around us, people and events around us."
>
> — *Carl Jung*

One day as I was leaving a networking event and about to begin the 45-minute drive home, I stopped to check my emails to make sure that all was well with my clients. I was dismayed to see an email from a current client who had been triggered by a fight with her best friend. Since we had been working together for a few months, I was well aware of the past trauma patterns my client had experienced and that her conflict with her best friend had triggered some of her trauma. My client and her friend were more like sisters than friends since they had known each other for over 30 years. And yet, my client was done with her friend's behavior. She was ready to toss the friendship. This was a relationship that needed to be saved, not thrown away.

I immediately called my client and as I drove, I spoke with her about the concept of "Perception is Projection".

As we began our conversation, she was quite sure that the relationship with her friend was not worth saving, but she was willing to do the process with me.

After a few minutes, my client realized that her friend was giving her the gift of knowing what was out of balance in her. She realized that she needed to take action to make changes, and this exercise helped her get clear on what she needed to change in herself. It was not her friend!

That evening, my client had a good heart to heart conversation with her friend and they had a loving resolution.

The 30-year friendship and sister love had endured this conflict, and their bond became much stronger after this.

Carl Jung, the Swiss psychiatrist and psychoanalyst, once said, "Projections change the world into the replica of one's own unknown face." Let that sink in for a second. It means the way you see the world isn't about what's out there, it's about what's *in here*, what's in you.

Jung's concept of "Perception is Projection" reminds us that what we experience externally is often a reflection of what's happening inside us. It's like looking at the world through a lens crafted by your own unconscious thoughts, feelings, and desires.

Let's break it down:

1. Projection

Jung believed that we unconsciously project parts of ourselves, our thoughts, emotions, and even aspects of our personality, onto the people and situations around us.

Here's an example: if you're carrying unresolved anger, you might see hostility in others that isn't really there. Or, if you're feeling insecure, you might assume others are judging you when they're not. These projections can be both positive and negative. The key is recognizing when what you're seeing in others is actually something within yourself.

2. The Influence of the Unconscious Mind

Here's where it gets wild: your unconscious mind is constantly shaping your perceptions, and you're not even aware it's happening. It's packed with personal experiences, repressed memories, and deep archetypal symbols that color your view of the world.

In other words, your unconscious mind is like a DJ spinning tracks behind the scenes, and those tracks influence how you experience reality.

3. Subjective Reality

This concept also highlights just how *subjective* reality really is. Your inner psychological landscape, the beliefs, emotions, and past experiences you carry all act like a filter. It determines how you interpret and react to what's happening around you. Two people can go through the exact same situation and walk away with completely different perceptions because their inner filters are different.

4. The Power of Integration and Self-Discovery

Here's the good news: projections aren't just about pointing out what's wrong, they're also a goldmine for personal growth. Jung saw identifying your projections as the first step to understanding yourself on a deeper level.

When you notice a strong reaction to something or someone, ask yourself, "What does this say about *me*?" By recognizing and owning your projections, you can integrate those unconscious parts into your conscious mind. This process is like peeling back layers of an onion, revealing your true self.

"Perception is Projection" reminds us that reality isn't purely objective. What you see in the world is heavily influenced by what's happening inside you. The way forward? Start paying attention to your reactions, assumptions, and judgments.

When you notice yourself getting triggered by someone's behavior or feeling drawn to a certain quality in another person, stop and ask:

- "What does this say about my own fears, desires, or beliefs?"
- "Am I projecting something unresolved onto them?"

This isn't about blame, it's about awareness. The more you understand your projections, the more self-aware and empowered you become.

Your external world is often a reflection of your internal one. Understanding "Perception is Projection" isn't just about seeing things differently, it's about *changing* the lens through which you see the world. When you do, you'll find greater self-awareness, deeper connections, and a more balanced relationship with life itself.

So, the next time something in the world rubs you the wrong way, or lights you up, pause and ask: "What's this revealing about *me*?" That's where the real growth begins.

Below is the process to help you to uncover what you may be projecting onto others and what you may need to do to shift your perspective and your projection.

Start by thinking of the person and all the traits or behaviors that bother you about that person. Write them all out in column A.

Remember the presupposition that "all behaviors have a positive intention". Consider each behavior that you wrote down in column A and *imagine* what positive intention the other person may have for their behavior. This often requires a big stretch and imagination.

Then, as this process is about your perception, it's time to energetically thank the other person for their behaviors and how much they trigger you and then ask yourself if you need more or less of the intention that you listed in column B.

Simply write out a "+" or "-" in column C.

Now, fold the page over so you no longer see the traits or behaviors of the other person. Looking at the positive intentions in column B, ask yourself what action plans you will put in place to either increase or decrease what is out of balance inside of you.

Then, visualize the face of the person who originally triggered you and send them an energetic message of heartfelt appreciation. It was your unconscious mind that was projecting what was out of balance inside of you. It's not them who is the problem, they are a gift for you to change.

A	B	C	D
Their Traits or Behaviors that Bother You	Positive Intention	+ or - (More or Less?)	Action Plan: What do you need more or less of?

For a great example of the Perception is Projection clearing technique, skip to Millionaire Code 5 – The Transformer to see Sara's example.

Clients who've gone through this process report back to me that the behaviors that used to drive them nuts about the other person no longer even phase them.

This is a powerful process that reveals so much about an individual and is so enlightening.

So, the next time you find that someone else's behavior is driving you crazy, or making you mad, pull this exercise out before you decide to avoid them forever or sever the relationship.

Anxiety

Several years ago, I sat down with a young woman named Catarina, who was gripped by constant anxiety. As we talked, it became crystal clear what was going on—her mind was stuck on a loop of worst-case scenarios. She was constantly imagining terrible things happening in her future.

Of course, she felt anxious! How could she not?

One of the foundational principles of NLP is this: *Anxiety is a signal from your unconscious mind to shift your focus to what you want.* Catarina wasn't just feeling fear; she was *visualizing it*—living in a mental movie of terror and problems. No wonder she was caught in a constant state of anxiety.

I walked her through a powerful NLP technique designed specifically to tackle anxiety. It's a simple yet transformative process that helps your mind rewire how it reacts to those fear-based thoughts.

And guess what? By the time we were done, Catarina's anxiety levels had dropped significantly. She learned how to shift her focus, break free from the cycle, and start visualizing a future that felt safe, calm, and in her control.

Anxiety isn't something you have to live with forever. You just need the right tools to turn it into a signal for growth instead of a barrier.

According to Psychology Today here is the definition of Anxiety.

"Anxiety is both a mental and physical state of negative expectation. Mentally it is characterized by increased arousal and apprehension tortured into distressing worry, and physically by unpleasant activation of multiple body systems, all to facilitate response to an unknown danger, whether real or imagined."

The NLP technique for clearing anxiety is delightfully simple and easy to remember.

First, ask yourself what it is *specifically* that you're feeling anxious about?

What specific event in the future are you feeling anxious about?

There's a part of you that thinks it's important for you to have some anxiety to motivate you. While it's important for you to be motivated, there are better ways to do this. Once again, anxiety is a warning from your unconscious mind to focus on what you want.

The problem is that anxiety is not good for the body.

Ask yourself, are there other ways that would be OK for you to motivate yourself, and let the anxiety go?

You must get permission from your unconscious mind to release the anxiety.

Clearing Anxiety

1. First, pick a specific event that is making you feel anxious.
2. What are you anxious about? What specifically?
3. Close your eyes, and just float out into your future to 15 minutes after the *successful* completion of the event about which you thought you were anxious.
4. Stay up above the event and turn and look toward now.
5. Now, where's the anxiety? That's right! It's disappeared.

6. At this point, from above the event, look down at yourself and imagine the best possible outcome. Make it positive. See yourself sighing with relief or smiling and nodding happily. Imagine yourself in the scene having a positive experience.
7. Come back to now. Float down into now and open your eyes.

This anxiety technique only works when you are thinking about one specific event in the future.

Clearing General Anxiety

Some people find that they feel general anxiety and try to do this for multiple future events at the same time. This technique won't work for that type of anxiety. If this describes you, then here's how you can get some relief from anxiety.

Remember, anxiety is a warning from your unconscious mind to change your thoughts and focus on what you want.

1. Close your eyes and turn within. Feel into your anxiety and ask your unconscious mind, what specific event are you anxious about.
2. Be patient, listen to the answer. It may come up as an image or a feeling. You might remember an event that happened in the past. Allow yourself a few minutes to get an idea of what you're feeling anxious about.
   a. If it's a past event, then your unconscious mind may be focused on the anxiety of that happening in the future. Follow the process above now that you have a specific event that you're feeling anxious about.
   b. If you get an image, then your unconscious mind may be conveying that you're feeling anxious about that. Think of a specific time in the future when something like that may

happen again. Follow the process above now that you have a specific event.

c. If your unconscious mind is persistent and just feeling anxious in general, then you'll need to reach out to an NLP Coach for further assistance. In the meantime, pay attention to your thoughts and imagine your future events to be positive.

You can reduce your feelings of anxiety by imagining your future as positive. Instead of imagining future events having negative outcomes, instead, see yourself in the picture and it going well. Imagine people nodding and leaning in. Imagine people loving what you're doing or saying. See how this shifts your anxiety levels.

Imposter Syndrome

I met Emma at a conference. The presenter was sharing how limiting beliefs will keep you stuck and need to be reprogrammed in your unconscious mind.

Emma asked, "Great! How do I do that?"

The presenter said, "Well, you need to work with an NLP Practitioner."

I was sitting at the same table as Emma. She turned to me and said, "Can you help me?"

Emma had already attained success as a 6-figure business owner. She loved what she was doing and was crystal clear on her niche. She was working with a really cool client and yet, right before a workshop with the executive team, she realized she was experiencing more than healthy nerves before a big client presentation. She realized that she was freaking out. So, she decided to dig deeper.

She recognized that she had some self-limiting beliefs around Imposter Syndrome that were stopping her from charging more for her services and expanding her business. She tried affirmations and visualizations and knew she needed more help to break through that invisible feeling and get to the place she wanted to be in the business.

During our time together, Emma discovered so much about herself. She discovered how to connect the dots between reactions and her emotional responses to all areas of her life and connect them back to beliefs she set when she was a child.

The coaching helped her to get greater context around her behaviors. She was amazing to see how her childhood beliefs had a hold over her in her life and business. She loved finding and clearing the original sources of her beliefs so she could see the waterfall of changes that she has experienced today.

Emma has been showing up more in her business. She used to have a lot of fear around visibility. She was terrified of posting on social media and didn't show up as much as she knew she could. That just went away.

Today, she is so fine with posting on social media. The fear went away, and she started to believe in herself more. Started to attract bigger ticket clients and really multiply her revenue. She tripled the value of her engagement and invests in herself more today.

She cleared the path to her 7-figure business and today is loving her life, her business and her family. She is well known for her brilliance and recently published her best-selling book.

Have you ever caught yourself drowning in self-doubt, fearing failure, battling negative self-talk, or feeling completely disconnected from others? Maybe you've been stuck in a cycle of self-sabotage or struggling with low confidence. Sound familiar?

Here's the truth, you're not alone. Let's crack open the reasons why you're doing it and, more importantly, show you how to stop.

Too many smart, successful people are secretly holding themselves back. Why? Because their minds are running on a constant loop of fear, limiting beliefs, and negative thoughts. They don't speak up in meetings. They play small instead of standing out. They second-guess their ideas. All because they don't fully believe in themselves.

If you've ever felt like you don't belong, like a fraud, or that you're not good enough, you might be dealing with *Imposter Syndrome.*

And guess what? You're in good company. Imposter Syndrome is that nagging feeling that you're not as capable or special as others think you are, and that any minute now, someone's going to find out.

Here's the secret truth. Imposter Syndrome isn't all bad. It can actually light a fire under you, pushing you to create, innovate, and show up in ways you didn't think possible. But when it's left unchecked? It can wreck you. Sleepless nights. Short temper. Constantly questioning your skills and worth. At its worst, it can lead to anxiety, depression, and even serious health issues.

The good news? You can take back control. Understanding Imposter Syndrome is the first step. It's a psychological pattern where you doubt your accomplishments and fear being exposed as a fraud. But here's the truth: you're *not* a fraud. You're human. You can flip the script on those fears to fuel your confidence and unlock the success you deserve. Let's get to it.

Imposter Syndrome is also known as:

1. Imposter Phenomenon
2. Imposter Experience
3. Inferiority Complex

Symptoms and Behaviors of Imposter Syndrome

1. Perfectionism
2. Procrastination
3. Constantly seeking to improve because you feel you don't know enough
4. Negative Self Talk/ Self Sabotage
5. Low self confidence, low self esteem, low self worth
6. Feeling out of your depth
7. Feeling undeserving of your success

8. Disconnected from others
9. Feeling alone, or like an outcast
10. Disappointment in yourself and your abilities
11. Unable to hear or receive positive feedback
12. Constantly comparing yourself to others
13. Not sleeping well, waking up in the middle of the night worrying
14. Having a short fuse, losing your temper quickly
15. Self doubt
16. Questioning your knowledge, skills and ability.
17. Feeling like a fraud
18. Not good enough
19. Not worthy
20. Worry
21. Anxious
22. Fear of failure
23. Anxiety
24. Depression

Dr. Pauline Rose Clance and Dr. Suzanne Imes at Georgia State University first identified the Imposter Phenomenon in the early 1970's when they were working with high achieving women. In 1978, they published a paper titled *"The Imposter Phenomenon in High Achieving Women: Dynamics and Therapeutic Intervention."* Initially, this phenomenon was observed in women, but over the years, Dr. Clance expanded their research, identifying the Imposter Phenomenon in up to 75% of individuals across diverse demographics. While it was first recognized in women, it soon became evident that many people, regardless of gender, resonate with these feelings.

Dr. Clance states that Imposter Phenomenon "Occurs among high achievers who are unable to internalize and accept their success. They often attribute their success to luck rather than to ability and fear that others will eventually unmask them as a fraud." See that? High achievers!

You may be surprised to hear who has admitted to having thoughts linked to Imposter Syndrome.

Some famous people who have experienced this are Author, **Maya Angelou** who stated "I have written eleven books, but each time I think, Uh oh, they're going to find out now. I've run a game on everybody and they're going to find me out."

Albert Einstein confided to a friend saying, "the exaggerated esteem in which my life work is held makes me very ill at ease. I feel compelled to think of myself as an involuntary swindler."

Alex Trebek, host of Jeopardy, in a TV interview in July 2020, stated. "I've been very lucky. Luck is a very important element in many people's success although they don't realize it."

In other words, if you've ever felt like an imposter, you are not alone. Many, smart, talented, successful people have felt symptoms of Imposter Syndrome at some point in their life.

How did it start?

In childhood.

As a child you often look up to your elders. Your parents, siblings, teachers, coaches, mentors, other kids in school, the neighbourhood, the list goes on.

Imposter Syndrome is often linked to how you were parented. If you were told you'd never be successful, or if you were told your grades were never good enough. I've had a few clients, myself included, who came home with a report card or test score and their well-meaning loving parents asked why they didn't score higher.

Imposter Syndrome begins as a seed of self-doubt, an inkling that you are not as good as another person and if this thinking continues because of experiences, you will start to program your unconscious mind with doubts. How you internalized the comments, jokes, and feedback from others will impact your degree of Imposter Syndrome.

You will believe everyone else is smarter, better, faster, more talented. You'll program your Reticular Activating System (R.A.S.), your brain's gatekeeper, into seeking out and finding proof that you are an imposter, a fraud, not good enough.

Constantly comparing yourself to others. Not acknowledging that others may have worked as hard or harder than you have to achieve the same results. Not acknowledging that others have negative thoughts and fears. In other words, comparing your "blooper" reel to their "sizzle" reel.

One might speculate that Imposter Syndrome comes up later in life as a way to ensure that you'll never be accused of overestimating your capabilities.

What is the solution?

1. Change Your Self Talk: Pay attention to how you speak to yourself. Identify your thoughts. Pay attention to what you say to yourself. Pay attention to your feelings or emotions that are coming up. Make sure your self-talk is positive. As Brian Tracy stated: "You are not what you think you are, but what you think, you are."

2. Accentuate the positive. Focus on what you've accomplished that you are pleased with. Keep a list or folder or file of positive

feedback and comments and refer to it often. Remember your wins.

3. Receive positive feedback. Be open to receiving positive feedback. Allow yourself to receive.
4. Learn from your mistakes. Reframe mistakes into learning opportunities. Discover the learnings and do better next time.
5. Define your criteria for success: Let go of being perfect – "nobody can relate to perfect". It's about meeting expectations. One of my colleagues didn't think she was successful in her business, then looked at her numbers and realized she had surpassed her annual goal.
6. Take Action Now: Do it now. Follow the 4 D's – Do it now, Diarize, Delegate or Delete the task. Action is the antidote to many fears.
7. Seek evidence of success. Measure it, celebrate it, remember it. I am a star because.. I am successful because ...
8. Reach out. Talk to a mentor or a coach and ask them to provide you with an objective external perspective of your performance.

Check out the Imposter Syndrome Assessment on the Millionaire Codes Portal at https://millionaire.codes

Reshma Saujani nailed it when she said, "Imposter Syndrome is just two made-up words on a page." She's right—it's a label, not a life sentence.

It's not about fighting Imposter Syndrome or fixing it. It's about flipping the script and using it. Let it fuel you when it pushes you to step up. But, and this is key, you've got to notice when it's not serving you.

If you're lying awake at night overthinking, snapping at people, holding back your brilliant ideas, or shrinking yourself to stay invisible—that's your sign. It's time to stop white-knuckling it and reach out for help. You're not supposed to do this alone.

Parts Integration

Let's talk about Parts Integration, a game-changer from NLP. It's all about clearing up the chaos in your mind so you can feel whole and invincible. Sometimes, a part of you gets stuck. Maybe it's that voice saying, "Don't try this, you'll fail," or the part that's working overtime to keep you safe but is actually holding you back. That part? It thinks it's running the show, acting in your best interest, but it's just draining your energy and creating conflict.

Here's the magic of Parts Integration, when you invite the part to join the whole of your unconscious mind, you reconnect and release that stuck part, and you unlock a flood of mental and emotional resources. Decision-making gets easier. Taking action feels natural. And suddenly, you're aligned with your goals instead of feeling like you're battling yourself every step of the way.

This isn't just fluff. Every NLP tool is designed to bring you back to wholeness and be in control. It's like hitting the reset button on your inner conflicts. You stop spinning your wheels and start driving forward, full speed, toward what you want. That's the kind of clarity and momentum we're talking about. Are you ready to reclaim those pieces of yourself and get back in the driver's seat?

First, a story.

Several years ago, I was reflecting on the concept of parts to find a personal example so that I could easily illustrate how parts come into being and create havoc with a person's behavior over their lifetime.

Upon reflection, I started to be aware of a pattern of behavior in myself as I was growing up.

The first event I remembered was a time when I was very little girl. I was in the bathtub with my sister, who is two years younger than I am, and the bathwater was starting to cool. I remember being so small that I could just see over the edge of the tub. When I was small, parents would leave their children in the tub. This was perfectly acceptable at the time. My parents were just down the hall with their friends.

I was aware enough that I couldn't get us both out of the tub.

I started to call for my mother.

"Mooooooooooom"

After a few calls, there was no response. I tried to call for my father.

"Daaaaaad"

Again, no response.

I tried again to call for my mother. Still, no response.

Now, we were starting to shiver as the water was getting cooler and cooler. Clearly, I wasn't being heard. I needed to ramp something up to their attention.

So, I called more loudly and with more emotion.

"Mommy!! Mommy!! Mommy!! Mommy!! Mommy!!

Suddenly, my parents and their friends were crowded in that tiny bathroom.

Hey! That worked!

A part was formed in my unconscious mind.

Another incident I remembered was my 7th birthday party. We were downstairs in the basement playing. None of the girls were paying attention to me so I started to cry to get their attention.

Suddenly, everybody was paying attention to me.

Hey! That worked!

The part got bigger.

Fast forward to grade five. I had written a speech and was looking forward to winning the writing contest in the school because I had been selected as a finalist the previous year.

When my speech didn't get selected for the next level of competition and I wouldn't be going on stage in front of the whole school, I went into the bathroom and started to cry. My teacher found out that I was very sad because I didn't get the attention I had expected and crying, he made the decision that I could go on stage.

Hey! That worked!

The part was getting even bigger now.

Throughout high school and into my first job in my 20s, whenever I wasn't getting the attention I wanted, I would start to cry.

The part grew and grew.

Consistently, I would get the attention I desired. Every time I ran this behavior, the part was getting confirmed that this pattern of behavior was getting my needs met and it worked well.

As you can imagine, it was not appealing to see a woman in her twenties, thirties and yes, forties crying because she wasn't getting the attention she wanted. This behavior was repelling people, but I didn't know why. The behavior was outside of my conscious awareness.

This pattern of behavior continued to work until one day I was in my corporate role, managing a team of people, and I was crying about a situation to my new boss. The Director of HR walked in as I was crying. She looked at me with disdain and turned to my boss and said "Oh, you've got a crier."

Not long after that I was fired for my behavior.

Hey! That's not working anymore.

By this point in my life, it was starting to believe that it was running the show.

The part that had formed in my unconscious mind at a very young age was that I needed to cry to get attention. In other words, to get my needs met, I needed to have an extreme crying response. Every time my needs were met in this manner, the part strengthened. This behavior was getting my needs met.

The more that the part was triggered and the more it worked to get the attention or result I desired, my needs were consistently being met and the part became bigger and stronger after every event.

This is what's happening for you if you have a behavior that you don't like but it's working. Your unconscious mind is growing the part to get your needs met.

Another way that I use to describe when a part is engaged is when you observe someone who is suddenly behaving like a kid.

You've heard about someone's behavior being described as "All of a sudden, she threw a tantrum like a 2-year-old." Or, "She started to cry like a baby." This is because the person is stuck in their part and the neurology that they are running has gone back to the time it formed and they begin acting that age again. The part has convinced them that this is how to get their needs met.

Two principles of NLP are important to state again here.

- One is that your needs are not negotiable. Your unconscious mind is constantly working on your behalf to ensure your needs are met. This is a biological and evolutionary need.
- The other principle is that all the techniques of NLP increase wholeness and choice.

So, you can see that parts that are formed in the unconscious mind are always in conflict. While the part is ensuring your needs are being met, they are going about it in an incongruent manner as they are not in wholeness and there is no choice.

This is why integrating the parts will improve your physiological energy and your psychological health. You will feel so much energy, ease, and flow when the parts are no logging hogging resources and getting you to behave in manners that make you cringe about afterwards.

Reconnecting to Your Wholeness

In the world of NLP, a "part" refers to a specific piece of your unconscious mind that has become disconnected from the whole. Think of it as a rogue team member, hogging resources and slowing down progress. While it's trying to help, its disconnection can create blocks in your nervous system, keeping you from functioning at your best.

Let's break it down:

What Are Parts in NLP?

1. A Problematic Disconnection
2. When a part becomes disconnected, it stops functioning as part of the whole. Instead, it acts independently, often creating problems, like a glitch in your nervous system.

3. Blocked Access to Resources
4. When a part is stuck, it hoards the resources associated with it. This block can limit both your physical energy and your emotional well-being, leaving you feeling out of sync or depleted.
5. It Thinks It's Helping
6. Here's the surprising part (pun intended): even when it's causing issues, the part believes it's acting in your best interest. It's convinced it's doing the right thing, completely unaware that it's disconnected from the bigger picture.
7. Wholeness Is Key
8. Your unconscious mind operates best when it's fully integrated. When parts work together as a whole, information and energy flow smoothly, supporting both your mental and physical health.
9. The Power of Integration
10. When a part is reintegrated, all the resources it's been holding onto are released back into your neurology. This boost can unlock energy, clarity, and alignment, helping you feel whole again.

How Parts Show Up in Your Life

1. Behavioral Patterns
2. Parts often manifest as behaviors that don't align with your goals. Ever find yourself reacting in ways you regret? That's likely a part at work.
3. Values and Beliefs
4. Each part carries its own values and belief systems, which can conflict with your overall goals. For example, one part of you might want to take bold action, while another part clings to safety, keeping you stuck.
5. Incongruence and Conflict

6. The more disconnected parts you have, the more likely you are to feel internally conflicted. This can show up as procrastination, self-sabotage, or indecision.

Why Integration Matters

1. Reduce Conflict
2. The goal of NLP is to reduce these internal conflicts. When you integrate your parts, you create harmony within yourself, allowing you to act with confidence and consistency.
3. Unlock Your Potential
4. By clearing blockages in your nervous system and reintegrating parts, you free up the energy and resources you need to move toward your goals.
5. Increase Choice
6. Parts integration increases your sense of wholeness, giving you more options to respond to life in ways that align with who you truly are and what you want to achieve.

When your unconscious mind is fragmented, it's like trying to drive a car with the brakes and accelerator pressed at the same time, exhausting, frustrating, and ineffective. Parts integration in NLP helps you take your foot off the brake, release what's holding you back, and reconnect with the full power of your unconscious mind.

When you're operating with your unconscious mind as a whole, everything flows. Energy returns, clarity sharpens, and your behaviors start aligning with your goals. That's the magic of parts integration, and it's your path to real, lasting change.

Anchoring

Anchoring is one of the most powerful techniques used in NLP. The concept of anchoring is based on the work of Ivan Pavlov, a Russian physiologist who was best known for his work in classical conditioning, which laid the foundation for much of behavioral psychology. Each time Pavlov rang a bell, he paired it with showing dogs a steak. He noticed that the dogs would start to salivate when they heard the bell. Eventually, just the sound of the bell made the dogs salivate, as if a steak were right in front of them. Pavlov's experiment showed the power of stimulus-response: the bell acted as an anchor, triggering a predictable reaction in the dogs.

Anchoring works the same way with us. When we're in a heightened emotional state, and a specific stimulus, like a sound, touch, or even a word, is applied consistently at the peak of that experience, the two become neurologically linked. This means that just by activating that stimulus, we can recreate the same emotional state over and over again.

Have you ever noticed that you have a certain response to a stimulus or trigger event? For example, when the doorbell rings, how do you respond?

Some people experience joy when someone is at the door. They immediately drop everything and make their way as quickly as possible to see who is there. Other people, wonder who could be there, they start to search their mind about a package or delivery they're expecting. They head towards the door with a sinking feeling of dread.

How interesting that a specific trigger – the doorbell ringing – creates completely different responses in people, don't you think?

Your brain is responding to different triggers in different ways all the time. Here is a list of triggers:

- Doorbell
- Telephone ringing/tone/vibration
- Text message notification
- Email notification
- Song
- Visual expressions
- And many more.

When your brain sees or hears a trigger outside of you, your brain immediately connects to an emotion based on the way your neurology has been programmed. Just like the two different responses to a doorbell ringing, your brain will respond the same way repeatedly.

Here's the good news. You can change the emotional response you have to an external event with anchoring.

Collapse Anchors Technique

Here's a great anchoring technique that you can learn and use for yourself whenever you don't like the emotion that comes up in response to a trigger. This is never, ever, ever to be used with a strong negative emotion, like anger, sadness, fear, hurt, guilt, terror, depression, rage, shame, grief or hate. This process is meant for milder negative emotions, like boredom, frustration, annoyance, irked, challenged, or confusion.

Here are some examples of when to use this technique:

1. You're experiencing a minor irritation.

2. You're feeling a bit nervous about a presentation or event.
3. You're not posting on social media or recording a video because of what someone might say or write.
4. You're not reaching out to invite people to work with you.
5. You're feeling stuck.
6. You're not taking action towards your vision.
7. You're worried about a new situation.
8. You're going to a family event and concerned about something happening or not happening.

Here's a simplified process to collapse anchors that you can use with yourself.

1. Stack Positive Anchors: Start by recalling a few powerful positive experiences. Think of times when you felt powerful, confident, and knew you could achieve anything. Anchor each one by putting them into your right hand, one by one, stacking them on top of each other.
2. Build the Positive Experience: Hold those positive experiences in your right hand. Notice what they look, feel, and sound like, imagine colours, sounds, textures, and shapes. Make a fist with your right hand and hold onto those powerful feelings.
3. Add the Negative Experience: Now, in your left hand, bring up the negative experience. If it's strong, hold it briefly without focusing too much on it; if it's not very strong, take a moment to notice its qualities (colour, sound, texture) as you did with the positive experiences. (Again, this is not to be used for a major negative experience or major negative emotion.)
4. Focus Back on the Positive: Revisit the feelings in your right hand, the positive experiences. Notice their brightness, strength, sound, and any other qualities. Let the positive feeling grow stronger.

5. Transfer the Positive Over the Negative: Slowly pour the positive experiences from your right hand into your left hand, layering in all the sounds, colours, and textures of positivity. If it helps, make a gentle "shhhh" sound as you do this. Continue until both hands feel balanced and the negative experience is fully diluted by the positive.

6. Seal It In: Clap your hands together once and rub them vigorously, mixing and reinforcing the new balanced feeling.

7. Confirm the Balance: Check to ensure both hands feel balanced and positive. If the negative experience still feels strong, repeat the process from Step 1.

To be guided through this powerful technique, follow the video in the Portal via https://millionaire.codes or via the QR code below:

Important Tips

Make sure your positive experiences are much stronger than the negative. This helps to dilute the negative with positive feelings, not the other way around.

Don't dwell on the negative feelings, keep them at a distance and focus on building up the positive.

This process helps you reduce the impact of minor negative experiences and strengthens your choice to feel empowered.

It's a powerful tool for letting go of what holds you back and creating a fresh neurological response to past experiences.

Part Three:
The Millionaire Codes

Millionaire Code 1:
The Clarifier

"What do you want?" the woman shouted at me. "What do you WANT!!" she escalated. "WHAT DO YOU REALLY WANT?!!!"

It was a month into the global pandemic of 2020, and I was attending a four-day leadership intensive on Zoom. The training started at 10:00AM and we'd been told it would run into the early hours of the morning. It was 11:30PM at the point the yelling began. I'm a big fan of sleep and not a big fan of screaming so my patience for this leadership training that my current coach required of her clients was treading on a thin nerve. However, this exercise was moving something in my heart.

The way it worked was that two of us were paired up in a zoom breakout room and were told to ask each other "what do you want" over and over with increasing emotion and intensity. The idea was to break each other out of the rote answers human beings tended to give and have us identify our truest and deeper soul desires. When I understood that I'd also be asked to scream this question at my partner, I'd moved my laptop into the basement so I wouldn't wake my husband and son who were sleeping upstairs.

I went into the exercise feeling pretty clear about what I wanted.

To be a bestselling author.

What do you want?

To be really, deeply, present with my son.

What do you want?

To continue having a great relationship with my husband.

What do you want?

To feel joy.

What do you want?

To know I gave every ounce of what I came here to give. To know I played full out. To move into a house we love that uplifts people and us. To write books that radically change people's lives for the better. To speak in a way that makes a real difference. To truly let go of unworthiness. To be the kind of leader that people like Maya Angelou and Elizabeth Gilbert have been for me.

My "what do you want" partner and I became friends after that night. She ended up writing a book with our team the next year, something that surprised her to hear coming out of her mouth during that midnight shouting session in the guest bathroom of my house.

Identifying, claiming, and clarifying what we really want is causative. This means that owning a vision, a goal, a desire- even before fully committing or taking action (the other codes will help with this), you set something exciting in motion. You send a flare up into the Universe and the Universe begins organizing itself to fulfill your dream. David Bayer, a favorite podcaster of mine, often says "desire + non-resistance = manifestation." In order to touch our true desire, we must tap into what we really want.

Remember Michelle- the high ranking military officer I saw at the first coaching conference I attended? The questions that helped her get clear on her desire led her lightening fast to commit to devoting her work to preventing military suicides. One of the first principles of NLP is to FOCUS ON WHAT WE WANT. This seems logical and hardly the need for an entire Millionaire Code until we consider what humans usually do: worry, stress, fixate, even obsess about what we don't want. Many scientists credit this perplexing phenomenon to what's called "the negativity bias." The National Institute of Health describes this as the way "adults display . . . the propensity to attend to, learn from, and use negative information far more than positive information." In her article on the topic, expert Kendry Cherry MSE, writes, as humans, we tend to:

- Remember traumatic experiences better than positive ones.
- Recall insults better than praise.
- React more strongly to negative stimuli.
- Think about negative things more frequently than positive ones.
- Respond more strongly to negative events than to equally positive ones.

In this first Millionaire Code, we arrest the negative bias and begin to prime the brain toward positivity.

Right up front, you get the opportunity to clarify what you desire and send a CLEAR signal to the Universe that you're ready to go by both naming it and releasing any initial resistance or subconscious fears that may try to stop or stall you from moving forward. Clarity and Alignment is what we're going for here. Once you activate this code, watch for signs and feel for intuitive nudges of what to do next. It wouldn't be unheard of for you to experience some rapid signs of progress or even manifestation just from doing this first code. Desire + non-resistance = manifestation.

Let's Goooo!

Answer these questions either in writing or with a partner. At each one, allow yourself to FEEL the emotions that accompany your answer. If you'd like us to guide you through this code go to the Portal via https://millionaire.codes or via the QR code below:

ESTABLISH THE DESIRE

1. What specific outcome, goal or dream, do you want to achieve?
2. Describe in detail what it would look like, sound like, and feel like when you have achieved this goal
3. When and where would you like to achieve/receive this?
4. What will be new/better/different when you've achieved this goal? For you internally, in your relationships, and in various areas of your life: finances, impact, what you're doing, relationships, and for the world?
5. Are there any potential downsides to having this?
6. How does this align with your top priorities and values?
7. What could possibly interfere with your ability to achieve/receive this outcome?

Or you could shorten this whole code to one sentence: WHAT DO YOU REALLY WANT?

Want to supersize the code?

Once you've reviewed your answers, ask:

BONUS: What's one bite sized action I could take today towards this goal/dream/desire?

Before you go to bed tonight: take the action.

Millionaire Code 2: The Emboldener

There was a point when I became really terrific at envisioning what I wanted. I could SEE the impact, the bigger stages, my books in bookstores and on the bestseller lists. I created vision boards with bright, exciting pictures of my vision. I said affirmations in the morning while I brushed my teeth. The future I desired played on a three dimensional cinematic loop in my mind. The problem was it all felt like a fantasy. Has this ever happened to you?

In the deepest part of my heart, I felt like there was a Grand Canyon sized chasm between where I was in reality and where I wanted to go. This is the code that built a bridge over that canyon. It's a great code to use when you feel insecure, uncertain and feel there is a large gap between where you are now and where you want to go. To prepare to activate this code

1. State the big goal or vision you want now.
2. Think of someone – an author, visionary, creator, or leader who has done what you want to do. Even better someone for whom this goal is EASY. For example, if you want to manifest $1Million, who is someone that sees a million as tiny - no big deal.

   Billionaires like Sara Blakely, the founder of Spanx, or Jamie Kern Lima, founder of IT Cosmetics, or Millionaires like Samia Gore, Founder of Body Complete Rx, or Vinita Rathi, CEO of Systango Technologies, to name a few examples.

Once you identify that person, you're ready to activate the code! [Note: as you go through the code, you can jot down your answers to the questions or turn on a voice recorder and speak your answers.]

To watch this in video format access the Portal via https://millionaire.codes or via the QR code below:

Start by affirming

I now give myself permission to have my vision board be my real life.

Next, ask

What would be the best part of that? What gets to happen for me that wouldn't happen if I let things stay exactly as they are? [feel free to write your answers]

How would I feel if I let myself have this goal?

What stops me from feeling that now?

Who is someone who is living the vision I want for myself? Great. Create a picture in your mind of that person.

Now, we always want to respect each person's energy, so imagine you can speak with that person's higher self. Ask the higher self of the other person if it would be okay for you to connect with the visionary you chose. If you feel a "yes", proceed with the code.

Now please imagine stepping into that person's experience - look through their eyes, as if you're seeing the world from their point of view, breathe with their lungs, and notice the thoughts they are thinking when they feel the most.

Now, ask yourself, what does this person believe about themselves and the world that has allowed them to achieve this success?

Notice all you can observe about their posture, their emotions, their vibration.

Write or speak any insights you have as you experience the world as this leader who has easily and repeatedly done what you want to do.

Now on the count of three, take a deep breath here, take all that you felt from this person and step forward into the version of YOU that has already, easily, and repeatedly done this vision. You did it! It worked! It's better than you imagined!

Really feel how it feels to know you've done it. Explore what is new, different, better in your world now that this vision is your reality. Write/speak what you see and especially how you FEEL.

Next, ask yourself, what do you now believe about yourself and the world, now that this is your new reality?

Now, look back at the you who started the exercise. The you some time in the past that wanted this thing that hasn't already done it. What guidance do you have for her?

What's the most important thing you want her to know?

Take a few deep breaths and write or speak what you hear.

Imagine now a golden light pouring over you. Imagine it activating this vision as your reality in every cell. Imagine filling with the power, confidence and beliefs of the leader you chose who went before you and the you who has already done this thing.

Know that you can return to this place and use this code in any moment that you feel uncertain.

Know that you are now feeling and acting like this person. It's already done.

Open your eyes if they are closed and determine one action you can take toward this vision in the next 24 hours based on the guidance of your future self or the beliefs and actions of the leader you embodied.

Commit to take this action and share it with another person.

Note to you from the Universe:
It was yours the moment you imagined it.

The first time I used a version of this code was with a colleague. We were both in the mastery coaching NLP based program, and we agreed to support each other by practicing the NLP sequences at least once a week.

Her vision at that time was to have a simple business, no team, no ads, not even a website. She wanted to make $200,000 a year doing deep, transformational work with a few people. She wanted to have total geographic freedom and be present in non-school hours with her two children.

She was a holistic healer which lends itself very well to the model.

My vision was to emerge as a high impact thought leader. I wanted to write bestselling books. Transform lives through speaking. I wanted to impact many 1000s of people a year through a powerful coaching company. The person I stepped into was Gabby Bernstein.

If you don't know Gabby, she's built an empire helping people connect with their spirituality in a hip fun way. She's authored multiple New York Times bestsellers. She sold out big auditoriums for her speaking engagements and workshops. She positively impacted many 1000s of lives a year all over the world.

As I stepped into Gabby that day, I felt a jolt. I felt expansive. What I heard through Gabby's eyes and heart and soul, is that she knew that what she did was needed in the world. She knew it was unique and valuable. And then when she wrote things, hosted events, and invited people to things, those things were wanted. She knew she was brilliant at public relations, branding and marketing. She knew how to impact on a global scale.

When I stepped into the version of me who had already created my vision, that future self told me "You're on the right path. Take the next big leap. Keep going. You will do this."

As simple as this exercise is, it changed things for me that day. Over and over when I felt insecure, small, that it was pointless, was besieged by all the Gremlins who told me no one wanted to hear what I had to say- I'm no one. A no name person, I thought about stepping into Gabby.

How did she think? What did she do? I tapped into Gabby's confidence, her conviction, her passion, her courage. This gave me momentum to take next steps. I took bigger risks. I reached out to people that I would have been horrified to reach out to and didn't take it personally if they never wrote me back. I started the Thought Leader Academy. I had the gall to pitch myself to bigger speaking engagements. I won a speaking contest and got featured at an event with a 1000 person audience. My books became bestsellers. Well, I have not reached the sort of legendary household name of Gabby, yet I know that resourcing her, stepping into her and activating her consciousness towards my own vision changed something. It shifted me further and faster than it would have if I'd just been thinking from myself.

After using the earlier version of this code, my colleague had her first six figure year. The next year, she made $200K without a website, while being with her kids every afternoon and weekend, with no team, 90% profitability here, and she and her family moved to the mountains, something they had always longed to do.

We are so excited for you to activate this code.

Vision Life – here you come!

To watch this in video format follow the video in the Portal via https://millionaire.codes or via the QR code below:

Millionaire Code 3:
The Accelerator

This code is ideal to use when you know exactly what you want, you feel a strong desire but you have no idea how you're going to make it happen. Or you want to accelerate the manifestation of your goal and have it happen EASILY.

When I was in high school, I watched *When Harry Met Sally...* countless times. It was funny with a tender, heartfelt core. By college, I knew pretty much every line of dialogue by heart. If you also love Nora Ephron (the brilliant writer of the film), and phrases like "days of the week underpants," "wagon wheel coffee table," or "singing *Surrey With a Fringe on Top* in front of Ira" mean something to you, then you get it. But there was one scene that no one else likely paid any attention to that I loved. It's later in the film. Harry and Sally are each dating other people, and they've met at their friend Jess' house for game night. Jess opens the door and says to Harry, "Hey, want to see the cover of my new book? It just got here."

I always became excited about this scene because I wanted deeply and profoundly to be a writer and thought how amazing and marvelous it would be to have a friend come over and be able to say my new book just arrived and walk them back to my writer's office to show them the cover.

What does this have to do with this code to your success?

This Code starts with you identifying a specific goal or dream, called an anchor image. Next, you choose an image (can be a single still picture or a mini moving scene) that represents the joy filled moment that your vision has manifested.

Your anchor image can be that clear moment of triumph: you receiving an award, standing on that red circle carpet with the TEDx letters behind you, seeing your book on the bestseller list, seeing the $100,000 in your bank account. It can also be a moment that represents when you fully take in the incredible manifestation you've received.

My goal in choosing an anchor image is to find something with the emotional charge that allows me to FEEL the joy/gratitude/relief/happiness/awe I will feel when this vision is manifested. To get there, I ask myself "what will I do the minute this dream is reality?" Your brain will offer up the perfect image or scene that puts you into the state of having that vision now (the goal of all manifestation practice.) So, when I got serious about becoming a successful, published author, it would be natural to choose seeing that bestseller seal on the cover of my book or the #1 new release tag on Amazon. I have since used those as anchor images for some of my books. But for my first book, I chose the anchor image of me welcoming a friend to my house and saying, "my new book just arrived - want to see the cover?" That moment inspired by the scene with Jess and Harry in the movie, brought up all kinds of feels. I envisioned this moment over and over while I started to write and kept writing and made revisions and finally found a writing coach and editor and pitched agents . . . I was filled with doubt every day, but I kept tuning my brain to that scene of me opening that door, seeing my friend's face filled with love and saying, "want to see my new book?"

Suzanne wrote more about this in Part II, but here's a quick refresh.

The concept of anchoring comes straight out of classical conditioning which was made popular with the now famous experiment by Ivan Pavlov, a Russian physiologist, who did an experiment with dogs that changed the game for behavioral psychology.

Every time Pavlov rang a bell, he showed the dogs a steak. At first, the bell was just noise, but over time, the dogs started salivating at the sound alone, even without the steak in sight. Why? Their brains had linked the bell to the delicious steak. That's the power of stimulus-response in action. The bell became an *anchor* that triggered the same reaction, every time.

This is the fun part; anchoring works the exact same way in humans. When you're in a heightened emotional state—think excitement, focus, or even stress—and a specific stimulus (like a sound, touch, or even a single word) is consistently present at the peak of that experience, the two get neurologically wired together.

Boom, connection made.

Later, just activating that stimulus can bring back that exact emotional state like clockwork.

Here's how it plays out in your daily life: when your brain catches a trigger—a song, a smell, a phrase—it instantly pulls up an emotion from your mental "playlist," based on how your neurology has been programmed.

The good news?

You can use anchoring to *reprogram* yourself and create emotions that serve you on demand. Imagine the possibilities!

Let's proceed with the Millionaire Code: The Accelerator

To do this code by video, go to the Portal via
https://millionaire.codes or via the QR code below:

1. Start by calling up a positive, emotionally charged stimulus that represents the fulfillment of your goal.
2. Connect that image or sound to the fulfillment of your goal but seeing/hearing it and generating the FEELINGS you will have when you achieve your goal.
3. Press your hand over your heart to anchor the thoughts and emotions there and hold it for up to 10 seconds.
4. Seal It In: Clap your hands together once and rub them vigorously, mixing and reinforcing the victorious feeling.

Repeat this process daily as you take action toward your goal.

The anchor image works for every kind of goal.

A few years ago, I was speaking at an event that I'd poured my heart and soul into creating. I wanted it to be a profit-generating event, but honestly, I couldn't see *how* that was going to happen. I had invested a lot into this event, and I was determined to deliver huge value. Deep down, I had this number in my heart: $200,000. That's what I wanted the event to generate.

But on paper, it didn't add up. I wasn't making a sales offer from the stage. And even if every single person in the audience enrolled in something, the numbers still wouldn't hit $200K. It just didn't make sense.

Instead of spiraling into discouragement, I decided to ask myself a different question: *What would I do? What would I feel if I actually received $200,000 from this event?*

The answer came to me immediately: I saw myself grabbing my phone and texting my accountability partner (AP) with a big, excited "OMG $200K!!!" text, loaded with emojis. That moment—texting my AP—became my anchor image. It wasn't even about seeing the money in my bank account; it was about the *joy*, the *gratitude*, the *relief* I'd feel in that moment of celebration.

From then on, every single day, I locked into that vision. While creating my presentation, rehearsing it during my walks, designing bold, colorful slides, and crafting a powerful workbook, I imagined sending that text. Over and over again, I saw it. I felt it. I believed it.

When the event finally happened, something *electric* took over. The energy in the room was off the charts. We were all cracked wide open, connecting at a level I couldn't have predicted. And here's the wild part: the event generated $200,000. Almost to the *penny*.

This wasn't about logic or spreadsheets. It was about vision, alignment, and showing up fully. When you anchor yourself to a feeling, a belief, and a clear vision, the impossible has a funny way of becoming your reality.

When I got my first book deal and was waiting for the launch, I still felt like I was making it all up. I wondered if I was dreaming or having a fantasy. Even when the TV and podcast tour was booked, I still questioned if I was really going to be a published author. Then the doorbell rang. There was a delivery. It was a three by two cardboard box of first edition hard cover copies of my book! My husband came home an hour later. I opened the front door, feeling Jess and Harry and Nora Ephron kind of merge into my body. "My new book just got here - want to see the cover?"

We've used anchor images to manifest new coaching programs, international trips and even to buy our dream homes.

Now, we are so excited for you to use this. We want to hear about the anchor image you choose. And then celebrate with you when that image becomes your reality.

To watch this in video format go to the Portal via https://millionaire.codes or via the QR code below:

Millionaire Code 4:
The Transmuter

Use this code if you know what you want but feel fear, resistance, doubt, imposter syndrome. I turn to this code almost every time I have a new goal. Why?

When you go after something new, big, exciting, or next-level, it's *completely normal* for fears, doubts, imposter syndrome, anxiety, overwhelm—even full-on panic—to show up. That's your brain doing its thing, trying to keep you safe by holding you back.

What's with this inner voice? It's been studied and called a lot of things over the years.

- Fritz Perls, the founder of Gestalt therapy, called it the *internal voice of judgment and criticism.*
- John Bradshaw, in his groundbreaking books on shame and unworthiness, labeled it the *inner critic.*
- Shirzad Chamine, author of *Positive Intelligence,* calls it your *saboteurs,* those self-sabotaging patterns of behavior that keep you stuck.
- Steven Pressfield nailed it in *The War of Art*—he calls it *Resistance.*
- And Rick Carson, in his classic *Taming Your Gremlin,* gave it a face—a *gremlin* that lurks in your mind, chipping away at your confidence and stealing your momentum.

No matter what you call it, it's the same thing: that voice in your head trying to stop you from growing, thriving, and stepping into your potential. But here's the truth—it's just noise. And you? You're in control.

Neuroscience has now explained the phenomenon that every writer, visionary, artist, entrepreneur, or leader, faces when they say yes to a next level goal. The reason we feel these uncomfortable and often derailing feelings is because of the amygdala located in the temporal lobe of our brain. The amygdala's job is to warn us and even inhibit us from doing ANYTHING it perceives as new, different, and/or bigger. This is because this part of our brain knows what we have achieved so far (this includes in health, money, impact, visibility, creativity, business) and we didn't die. The amygdala is in the business of SURVIVAL. So, if you've made $50,000 in a year and you didn't die, the amygdala wants you to only make $50,000 every year forever. And while it's true that whatever you've experienced in your relationships, health, finances and success did not kill you, staying right where you've been likely does not equal your full self-actualization, purpose, destiny and success.

The amygdala can't see the big picture. It's misinformed. It's well meaning but unenlightened. The good news in all of this is that we don't need to be afraid when this part of our brain freaks out as we contemplate or take action on our vision.

Just bring whatever RESISTANCE or gremlins you feel to this code and let it work its magic!

You'll need:

A piece of paper (you can type this, but you will access different parts of your brain if you hand write.)

Pen

Quiet space

If you'd prefer to do this along with a video where I guide you through the entire thing, go to the Portal via https://millionaire.codes or via the QR code below:

Write your next big goal or desire at the top of the page.

Then draw two vertical lines so you end up with three columns.

Say your goal out loud. Example: I now manifest $100,000. Or my book is now an international bestseller.

Take a few deep breaths.

Next, in the left column, write every reason your mind worries that you cannot be, do, or have that goal. Keep reading for a specific example.

This is not the time to be spiritual or write what we wish we thought or felt. This is the opportunity to let the gremlins rip. Be as specific as possible. Here's what I wrote when I first wanted to reach six figures per year as a coach:

COLUMN 1

I have no idea how to do it

The most I've made is $50K in year

Other people can do this but I can't

I don't deserve to make 6 figures

I'm not worthy of making 6 figures

It's greedy that I want this

I'm not good with money

Note: Every time I set a goal, I wish I'd felt confident and full faith/belief in my vision. Column 1 makes it completely ok and normal to have resistance. If you also fear and doubt yourself, you're not alone. Let's keep going so you can have a transformation!

In a more recent example, here is my left column when I set a goal to 100K subscribers on YouTube. I'll walk you through the entire code with this example.

Note: my starting point at the time of setting the goal was 1.6K.

GOAL 100,000 YouTube subscribers

COLUMN 1		
You're probably not capable of going to 100K+ YouTube subscribers		
I don't have the brand or audience to get to 100K		
People with 100K+ are Big Names		
I don't have the budget of people with 100K+ subscribers		
I don't have the high production quality or tech or studio of top YouTube thought leaders		
People want to watch famous people's YouTube content, not yours		
You're so egocentric - greedy to want 100K subscribers on YouTube		
People with big YouTube followings are lovable (and you're not)		

After you write the list of resistant thoughts, beliefs and ideas, it's time to let go of all that negative energy. Take a deep breath, roll your eyes up, stick out your tongue as far as possible and exhale forcefully through your mouth while making a "HA!" sound. This is called Lion's Breath, or *Simhasana* in yoga. It will release the negative energy, the limiting thoughts. and clear mental clutter. Repeat 3 – 5 times as needed to feel the release.

If you're still feeling fear, discouragement, or a strong attachment to the belief that the thoughts in Column 1 are true (trust me, I've been there too), join me in the Portal via https://millionaire.codes or via the QR code.

Together with a group of thought leaders, we'll guide you through a more powerful release technique using Emotional Freedom Technique (EFT), also known as tapping. Let's tackle this together for a deeper shift!

Writing down the thoughts in Column 1 can feel uncomfortable— maybe even a little like crap. But here's the good news: just by putting those thoughts on paper, you've already started to release them. You've taken the first step in dissolving those ideas.

Here's even *better* news: the only real thing standing between you and what you want? It's Column 1. We think it's about money, time, or other people, but nope. The only true blocks are in your subconscious mind. Column 1 is nothing more than a false story told by an unreliable narrator.

Remember what Steven Pressfield shared? He called it Resistance— and he's crystal clear: "*Resistance is always lying and always full of shit.*" That's exactly what's in Column 1: lies. Everything you write in that column is a lie.

And you know what? That's amazing! Because once you see it for what it is, you can stop believing it and finally move forward.

Once you've digested this, you're ready to move to column 2!

In the middle column- column 2 - write the opposite of each item in column 1.

Note: you do not need to believe what you're writing, just feel around until you find an opposite statement that creates a response of relief or possibility.

Here's my real example of Column 2 about the goal of reaching 100K subscribers on YouTube.

If you don't have personal experience to draw from, that's totally okay. You can find inspiration in someone else who started where you are and achieved what you want. According to quantum theory, there's only one unified field—one total mind—and we're all connected to it. Carl Jung called this the *Collective Consciousness*.

What works for one person can absolutely work for many when you align your energy with that belief. Their success is proof of what's possible for you, too.

COLUMN 1	COLUMN 2	
You're probably not capable of going to 100K+ YouTube subscribers	I didn't think I was capable of writing a book, getting published, being a bestseller, making 6 figures a year, then 7 figures a year and I've been able to co-create all those things and so many more so I could do a goal like 100K on YouTube	
I don't have the brand or audience to get to 100K	Creating content on YouTube will build my brand and audience- the channel can/will grow alongside my brand.	
People with 100K+ are Big Names	A big way people become big names is by creating great content on platforms like YouTube. Doing this work is the way to JOIN big names. To be big, I get to play big. This is the way.	
I don't have the budget of people with 100K+ subscribers	I have no idea what people's budgets are. I am resourceful. I will figure out, co-create and receive the resources I need. The Universe is my Source. I've created many things without a big budget including growing my business to $1Million with no ads or PR. I can do this!	
I don't have the high production quality or tech or studio of top	Heart, energy and value are more important than gear or tech. I can invest in higher quality production as I go. The most important thing is to SERVE people on this platform and make a difference. I can do that with the equipment I have.	

YouTube thought leaders		
People want to watch famous people's YouTube content, not yours	People are always looking for new inspiration, solutions, innovation and support. The YouTube algorithm suggests videos by TOPIC not just or even as much by audience size. There is room for me and all of us on this platform.	
You're so egocentric- greedy to want 100K subscribers on YouTube.	The videos and content I'm creating for YouTube is useful, relevant, strategic, and helpful. Plus, I'm activating my videos with neuroscience that will help it really make a difference and create transformation. Additionally, when I create great results on YouTube my clients and audience will benefit because I will share all I've learned. When people see me/leaders RISE, they get lifted up and can RISE faster too. I create WIN-WIN content so it's not selfish, it's a gift.	
People with big YouTube followings are lovable (and you're not)	This is the voice of my family, not the Universe. Like everyone, I am lovable. I'm unique. I have unique magic and value to share. My gifts, inspiration, ideas and talents are the Universe's gift to me and what I do with them - now to share them on YouTube - is my gift back to the Universe. It is my calling to do this.	

When you're written your Column 2 answers, read them out loud and observe how you feel. Better? Less resistance? Whatever you feel, congratulations on taking action! You've unhooked another level from the false story.

You're ready for the final part of the code!

To complete column 3, pretend a best friend shared her biggest goal and desire and showed you her column 1 list. You believe in this friend. You know she's amazing, you know she's powerful. You would likely almost laugh at that list because you'd know how capable, awesome and worthy she is to achieve it. You'd see possibilities. Likely, before she even finished reading her column 1 you'd be brimming with ideas and solutions for her. Now you're going to turn that love and genius on your goal. In column 3 write a list of a solution for each resistance point from column 1.

COLUMN 1	COLUMN 2	COLUMN 3
You're probably not capable of going to 100K+ YouTube subscribers	I didn't think I was capable of writing a book, getting published, being a bestseller, making 6 figures a year, then 7 figures a year and I've been able to co-create all those things and so many more so I could do a goal like 100K on YouTube	Daily affirmations: I am capable, worthy and built for building a massive following on YouTube. I'm called to this vision for a reason. What I am seeing is seeking me. Delivering value and contributing big on YouTube is my DESTINY.
I don't have the brand or audience to get to 100K	Creating content on YouTube will build my brand and audience- the channel can/will grow alongside my brand.	Find 5-10 people who did not have a big brand or following and built one on YouTube. Watch interviews, videos, read their books and find the common denominators. Implement all that are value aligned with you.
People with 100K+ are Big Names	A big way people become big names is by creating great content on platforms like YouTube. Doing this work is the way to JOIN big names. To be big, I get to play big. This is the way.	I am one with the top creators on YouTube. The reason I am called to this is because it's what the Universe wants to do with and through me.
I don't have the budget of	I have no idea what people's budgets are. I am resourceful.	Get actual #'s of what it will take to implement the

people with 100K+ subscribers	I will figure out, co-create and receive the resources I need. The Universe is my Source. I've created many things without a big budget including growing my business to $1Million with no ads or PR. I can do this!	strategies I discover in the first box of column 3. Identify anything I'd want to swap to give money to this goal. Play my 50 ways game to get inspired for ways to make $ for this investment. Envision
I don't have the high production quality or tech or studio of top YouTube thought leaders	Heart, energy and value are more important than gear or tech. I can invest in higher quality production as I go. The most important thing is to SERVE people on this platform and make a difference. I can do that with the equipment I have.	Research what production tech/gear/interior design I'd want. Make a vision board on Pinterest of the space and gear I want. Ask people I know if anyone has a space that's ideal for this I could rent inexpensively, or they are not using. Begin researching great editors and production team. Find out their rates. Envision my videos being and looking top world class and having a world class team working with me daily. Show up on video as if I already am and have top production quality. "Pretend" I already have the team and support I envision. SEE IT FEEL IT BE IT.
People want to watch famous people's YouTube	People are always looking for new inspiration, solutions, innovation and support. The YouTube algorithm suggests videos by TOPIC not just or	Start creating the highest value videos and content I can imagine - content that truly helps people.

content, not yours	even as much by audience size. There is room for me and all of us on this platform.	
You're so egocentric-greedy to want 100K subscribers on YouTube.	The videos and content I'm creating for YouTube is useful, relevant, strategic, and helpful. Plus, I'm activating my videos with neuroscience that will help it really make a difference and create transformation. Additionally, when I create great results on YouTube my clients and audience will benefit because I will share all I've learned. When people see me/leaders RISE, they get lifted up and can RISE faster too. I create WIN-WIN content so it's not selfish, it's a gift.	Bring my heart and soul to quantum magic to every piece of content. Share it with everyone I currently know. Invite others to learn and grow with me. Generously share all that works. Envision thank you comments and shares, subscribers, and watch hours that affirm people are loving the content and wanting more.
People with big YouTube followings are lovable (and you're not)	This is the voice of my family, not the Universe. Like everyone, I am lovable. I'm unique. I have unique magic and value to share. My gifts, inspiration, ideas and talents are the Universe's gift to me and what I do with them - now to share them on YouTube - is my gift back to the Universe. It is my calling to do this.	This vision is an amazing opportunity to break the cycle of this LIE from your family. It was never the truth that you're not lovable, it's not the truth now, and it will never be the truth. When you break this cycle, everyone has permission to break free from the lies they've believed. Reaching this goal is about so much more than YouTube - it will create a WIN WIN ripple that will benefit all.

Want to SUPERSIZE this code? Follow the video in the Portal https://millionaire.codes or the QR code below:

Here's how to supercharge this millionaire code and take it to the next level:

1. Anchor Your New Beliefs: Take your top one, two, or even all your new beliefs and make them impossible to ignore. Write them on sticky notes and put them around your workspace, tape them to your bathroom mirror, or make them your phone's screensaver. You can even set alarms on your phone with your new beliefs to remind yourself throughout the day. The more you see them, the more you integrate them.

2. Prioritize Your Actions: Look at the ideas and solutions you brainstormed for your challenge. First, sort them by what feels doable right now. Then, reorder them by which actions would create the biggest results the fastest.

3. Take Action Today: Pick *one* action from your list and commit to doing it in the next 24 hours. If it feels too big, break it down. For example, if one of your steps is to connect with your "Power 100," start with the first 10 names and reach out to at least one person today. The key is to get moving because action is the antidote to fear.

4. Get Accountability: Find a buddy or accountability partner to keep you on track.

Remember: The antidote to imposter syndrome is a new identity. The antidote to the old story is the *true story*—your new story. You've got this. We're beyond excited to see you put this into action and make it real. Let's go!

Millionaire Code 5:
The Transformer

We would love it if this code was not needed in this book. Who likes to be triggered? Experience setbacks, even betrayals or what our brain will label "failure?" Exactly NO ONE!

No one wants to put out a course, event, book, or product and have few to no one buy it/register

No one wants to have a team member fall short or worse, betray them

No one wants clients to ask for a refund or to ghost them

No one wants someone else to copy your work and never acknowledge that they've done this

No one wants to be judged or attacked online when all you are doing is putting heartfelt, valuable, high integrity work in the world.

Perhaps even reading this list is giving you the feeling of hives or making you want to stop reading and run from this book.

Please keep reading - we have something good coming - we promise!

The thing is, when we are alive, walking around on the planet and certainly starting business, working with other people, trying new things, this combination of uncomfortable situations and our reactions to them- what Sara calls Business PTSD, can arise.

The KEY is to know what to do if you experience this and the CODE to quickly and authentically TRANSFORM what feels like what our friend Molly Jones calls a "Shitnanigan" (shitshow + shenanigan) into a portal to massive growth and success.

Use this code for any upsetting, triggering situation to GET FREE! You'll know when it's time for THE TRANSFORMER when you feel yourself obsessively thinking about or feeling upset by a situation. When you feel shocked or betrayed by someone's behavior. When you feel like a victim (and have plenty of evidence to support that you are). When you feel stabs of guilt or a waterfall of shame. When you are in the quicksand of resentment. When you want to quit, run away, hide, to push the F-IT button on your business, disappear, go "get a job" and never hire, date, risk, or be vulnerable again.

We've got you!

Do The Transmuter and then pair this Code with the one in this book that most matches your next desired state (Success, Abundance, Freedom, Manifestation etc.) and you won't even be thinking about the thing that brought you to this code. In fact, even as you read this, it's going out the exhaust pipe and disappearing into the rearview mirror!

Before we do the code, we want to share a few things with you. 1. You don't feel alone if anything similar has happened in your life and 2. So the code itself will make more sense.

Sara

Early on in my career as an author-speaker-coach, I boosted my first post on Facebook. I'd been slow to get on social media (I wanted to spend my time writing books and serving my clients!) and I felt vulnerable starting to put invitations to my work out to the greater world. I made a post about a writing workshop I was hosting where people could learn the method I'd developed to write a book in 12 weeks. A day after posting (and spending $20 to boost my post) a family member texted me.

FM: "Is this you???" and she included a screen shot of the post.

Me: "It is!" I said, happy that the post was being seen.

FM: "A lot of my friends are on Facebook. This is really embarrassing for me."

What I remember in that moment was feeling surprised and then horrified. Here I'd done something new and uncomfortable (be more visible) and I'd upset someone I care about. The shame came on so hard and fast that I didn't even have enough voice to speak.

You may read this and think, what the heck is wrong with you Sara. Who cares if your family member didn't like your post! Just ignore her! Tell her she doesn't have to read it. Invite her to stop following you. Or maybe you would have been curious and asked a family member "what about this is embarrassing for you?" Or maybe you're thinking why didn't you tell them to f-off? These are all logical, rational responses and yet, in that moment, I wasn't reacting as a rational, logical adult.

Instead, I was smacked right back to my childhood where I heard frequent and resounding messages that I was "too much." In middle school, my parents sent my sisters and I to a youth group at our church. The group met Wednesday evenings and a couple from the church led the sessions. I found the conversations interesting and stimulating. They presented philosophy and world religions, and I was already captivated by spirituality. The rest of the group was less enthusiastic. I would often be the only person raising a hand to answer a question or share my thoughts on the reading. One day, after once again being the only person raising my hand to answer a question they'd posed, the wife of the couple lifted her arms in exasperation and said "OK Sara! Enough! We've all heard from you!"

I felt the room pause and swell. I pressed back in my chair, feeling shocked.

Then the laughter started. The other kids in the room started to snicker then build to full blown hysterical laughing. "We've heard from you! We've heard from you!" This was the phrase I heard for the rest of that year and years beyond. I stopped raising my hand after that. Even in college, for decades actually, I'd hear the inner critic join me at a party, on a masterclass, in a conference, at a party questioning if I'm talking too much, sharing too much, taking up too much space.

When that family member said she was embarrassed by my Facebook post, twenty years after that moment in the youth group room, I didn't react as a thirty something woman would behave. I was reacting as the young kid who'd been shamed into silence. I didn't get curious about why a Facebook post inviting people to a writing workshop would be embarrassing to someone. Or to my family member. I didn't. I couldn't. All I could feel was that I'd shared myself in a bigger way and it made someone upset. People "didn't want to hear from me."

I stayed off Facebook (and all social media) for five years.

This incident was so tiny. Not even a speedbump, a blip! It shouldn't have had any effect. And yet, because of the lens of my past, I let it send me running for the invisibility cave. I let it stop my voice.

I include this here because it is so "silly" logically. And while there's no mandate that I need to share on social media, I also know that hundreds of thousands of people I could really help write books, share their stories, their missions, their message, create legacies, change lives, and make millions of dollars ARE on social media. It served NO ONE for me to avoid social media and sharing my message for those years. When we break the LIE, everyone is liberated.

Maybe you, like me, have had a "minor" experience stop you from pursuing something important, something you desire, something you could be great at- something you were BORN TO DO!

Maybe you're working with something bigger. THE TRANSFORMER can be used for the "smaller" things all the way up to the capital T business traumas.

A few years ago, I brought someone into my business who came *highly* recommended. People I trusted—amazing people—raved about her. She had the credentials, the skills, the training. She even wrote one of the best proposals I'd ever seen. It was detailed, compelling, and painted a beautiful picture of what she would lead and contribute to our organization. I borrowed trust based on our mutual connections.

And then I over-delegated.

At first, it seemed like things were fine. A few months in, though, cracks started to show. She signed for things on behalf of the company—things I became financially responsible for. She reassured me, kindly but firmly, that "she was handling it," but in reality, she was making costly mistakes. She ignored requests in writing, approved expenses outside of her authority, and dropped critical balls.

When it was all said and done, between her salary and the financial fallout of her actions, I was out over $100,000.

And it wasn't just this one situation. At the same time, two other major financial surprises hit. There were industry changes, and my husband's business slowed to nearly a standstill. I couldn't sleep for months. I lay awake agonizing, wondering if I'd have to sell my car, move out of my house—completely upend my life.

The regret was overwhelming.

Why had I made this choice? How had I, someone who had run a *profitable* business with a strong cash reserve for years, gotten into this situation? I couldn't stop replaying it in my mind, wondering where I went wrong.

I called Suzanne and she whipped out this code. Her name for it was "Perception is Projection", which she explains in more detail in Part II of this book. I took one look and knew I didn't want to do the sequence. I was so angry. I felt betrayed. I felt shame. I knew there was much in my own delegation and management that contributed to this situation. I understood then where I'd been too assuming and laissez faire. I knew I would do it differently in the future (and have!) But in that moment, I stepped in the familiar quicksand of my childhood where I was both a victim and also believed that everything was my fault. I didn't want to do this code and "let it go." I also knew it would start to set me free.

NOTE: This is NOT the code to use when you are in the midst of an experience of business or other trauma. You'll want some distance before it is loving to use this code. It has always been crucial for me to get qualified 1-1 support to process, grieve, and do the inner work that is deserved and needed when we go through something big. Use this when your intuition says you're ready. When you are, it can create the SPACE to get out of "victim" and into "solution mode" - the genius zone that has the answers to use this situation to become your next BIG LEAP!

To do this code together, follow the video in the Portal via https://millionaire.codes or via the QR code below:

A	B	C	D
Traits or behaviours that drive you nuts	Intention (always positive)	Do you need more or less of column B?	Action Plan What do you need to do to achieve your goal of column C?

Here is what I wrote about the aforementioned situation.

COL A

Behaviors that drive me nuts:

Selfishness

Not taking responsibility

Not offering or being willing to help with a solution or contribute financially to the errors she alone made

Misrepresenting abilities and skills

COL B INTENTION (what was her imagined positive intention)

Put herself first

Getting her needs met

Being a Yes person/ wanting to handle things and give value

COL C (would it serve me to have more or less of anything column B)

MORE: putting myself first and getting my needs met

NOT: saying yes just to say yes and wanting to handle things above my skill level

COL D (what will I do to give myself what is good for me from column C)

I will put myself and my needs first by creating a new system to vet and qualify people with whom I work. I will create a training and oversight plan for any new positions. I will run all financial decisions (set up legally, enforced and signed by both parties in writing) for any collaborations I do. If I delegate financial decisions in the future, I will have regular review meetings to ensure best decisions are being made for the highest good and profitability of the company.

In the twelve months following this experience, we streamlined our team to a lean, high performing, value aligned, JOYFUL community with a clear, high vibe culture. We reconceived our business model and implemented a new strategic plan for growth. We rose in new sales, cash in AND grew our profits from 18% (the number we hit after the setbacks that year) to 60% within 12 months.

Millionaire Code 6:
The Shift

Use this Code if you:

1. Can't picture success in your current goal
2. You've tried going for your current goal before and it didn't work out
3. You're going for something really big, and your mind keeps pointing you into why it won't work

Rachel was a doctor, an unhappy one. She'd gone to medical school to please her parents. And even though she'd specialized in the kind of medicine - women's health - that lit her up she'd never been able to make what she considered a success of her career. What she secretly wanted was to be a writer, but believed with every part of her that this could never happen, that there's no way that she could pursue her passion, live her dream and actually make money.

Rachel had dutifully gone to her job for over ten years and had stopped when her second daughter turned five. Her days became filled with carpools, dance lessons and most recently preparing for her eldest's Bat Mitzvah.

She finally gave herself permission to take a writing class at an adult education center in Chicago. She enjoyed the classes, but the problem was she couldn't get herself to write, even though she created some time, got her girls into a carpool home from school three days a week.

She'd become increasingly frustrated, beating herself up.

The writing school brought me in to teach a workshop called "The Mental Game for Writers." I shared with the class that I'd wanted to be a writer since my grandmother gave me my first journal at five years old and yet, after that, for years, for over a decade, I had not been able to sit down and write anything.

Rachel grabbed me at the break. "I am where you used to be," she said. "I feel like a failure."

We began coaching. "Before we coach on the craft, accountability, making time to write," I said, "would you be open to doing a mindset exercise?"

"I'm not woo-woo," she said. "But at this point I'll try anything."

I told her the sequence I wanted to try was one that had created a big shift in my motivation - the one that cut through the self-doubt and failure gremlins that were yelling through a megaphone in my head every time I sat down at my computer. "It opened the floodgates," I said.

The Shift Strategy

I explained that right now, the neural pathway associated with writing was wired with "failure". This is happening in the subconscious mind and it's automatic. I shared that the thoughts and beliefs in the subconscious mind + our emotions determine 90% of our choices. We think we're choosing rationally, but most often, we're not.

"Our thoughts create our emotions which determine what actions we take which then determines our results." I drew this "equation" on a whiteboard in my office.

"What this strategy is designed to do is create a new neuropathway that associates writing with success. The aim is that this shift of association will get your writing - enthusiastically."

"I'm a doctor," Rachel said. "I'm not woo-woo. But okay."

I asked Rachel, if despite feeling like a failure and everything she tried professionally, there'd ever been a time when she'd felt successful? She sat for a long time, a few tears running out the outside corners of her eyes.

"I really can't," she said. "I got straight A's in school, but that was mostly because my parents forced me to and honestly it wasn't that hard. I didn't do anything great with medicine. Not like my friends who were chief residents. I didn't even make much money as a doctor at my OBGYN practice." Rachel was so strongly identified with a narrative of failure that she couldn't see the success of her fifteen-year marriage, raising her daughters, her creativity, getting into medical school or even the fact that she passed the medical boards exams, which are considered some of the most difficult in existence. None of the professional or academic achievements had brought her joy, none of it made her feel fulfilled.

"Just keep thinking back in your life - you can go back to early childhood," I said.

Rachel's face beamed. "This isn't a big deal or anything but one time . . ." she said. I urged her to continue. Whatever was making her smile like that was "it."

"I played soccer in middle school. And we went to regionals," she said. "And we won." Lisa was sitting up straighter. She leaned toward me with enthusiasm. She conjured the scene so well, I smelled cut grass, could sense the Babysitter's Club books in her backpack, and the sound of the referee whistle. "It was so great," she gushed.

"I remember the last minute, making a pass to my friend Jen who kicked it past the goalie. We were screaming and jumping around. We lifted Jen up on our shoulders - like they do at the Olympics!"

Rachel had her victory image. The memory that when just imagining, made her feel like a winner.

"What's the moment, on that day, that represents the whole awesome experience," I asked.

"When they gave us the trophy and we lifted Jen up in the air," she said. "The trophy was huge. Four pillars and two stories and all the gold and fake wood. That was the best," she said.

"You're ready for the shift strategy," I said.

The Shift Sequence

To be guided through this code, follow the video in the Portal via https://millionaire.codes or via the QR code below:

Select the goal that feels impossible - the thing you're afraid you can't be, do, or have. Pick a representation of that goal. For Rachel, it was sitting down to write and no words coming out, her shoulders hunched, and her head hanging down like Charlie Brown.

Then select a "victory" scene like Rachel did with the regional soccer win and the exact image: holding up Jen and the trophy. Note: if you have trouble like Rachel did or can't think of anything that excites you, you can "borrow" a victory image from something you've seen in the world or a movie. If you want to imagine Taylor Swift blowing kisses to the audience on stage for the ERAS tour, by all means, go for it!

Then, imagine the Victory Image in front of you and answer the following questions:

Is the image moving like a movie or still like a photograph?

Is it color or black and white?

How big is the image or movie?

Does it have a border or frame?

Notice the answers to these questions and lock that scene/image into place mentally.

Next, bring the goal image to mind. Ask yourself the same questions:

When you imagine your goal image,

Is the image moving like a movie or still like a photograph?

Is it color or black and white?

How big is the image or movie?

Does it have a border or frame?

Then, change the goal image into the exact specifications of the victory image.

For example, if the victory image is in motion like a movie, make the goal image match it. If the victory image is in color and the goal image is black and white, make them both color. If the victory image was huge and panoramic, make the goal image the exact same size and shape. If the victory image has a border but the goal image does not, but a border around the goal image.

Now for the shift in the brain.

Place both (now matching) images, side by side. Imagine sliding the goal image behind the victory image.

Bring them back side by side.

Then, say the word "SHIFT" and slide the goal image behind the victory image. Do this ten times saying "shift" every time you slide the goal image behind it. See the victory image begin to shimmer as it absorbs the goal image into its light.

Note: Your analytical brain may think that this is a silly exercise and it won't make any difference. Here's the thing with this, and all these techniques, the more you surrender to the process and the belief they will work, the more they do work. Simply surrender and believe.

So, if you've read this far, do it anyway! After you've "shifted" ten times let the images fall away.

Sit quietly for 1 minute.

Notice if you feel any differently. You may notice tingling, a lightness or not notice anything physical or emotional at all. Any shift is the sign that the neural pathways in your brain are shifting to create new habits, beliefs, and responses.

The great thing to remember is that you don't have to sense any change at the time of doing the shift. You can trust (or act as if you trust) that something has moved and that you will think/feel/act differently as a result.

After doing the shift strategy, Rachel did write her book. She's written two so far. She had several articles published in her local paper. She was offered a regular column. And like she'd wanted, dreamed and hoped, writing eventually became her new career.

Millionaire Code 7:
The Peacekeeper

Nel was doing quite well in life. She was living her passion of running a successful video production company and watching her business expand, even during the pandemic.

However, something was nagging at her that she was just not enough. She felt she was not getting credit where credit was due.

At the same time, she was nervous about showing too much ego and was working hard to keep humble.

Nel knew that she wasn't setting the firm boundaries she needed to but she felt she just couldn't. She told me that she felt bad and continuously apologized when she spoke up and asked for what she needed.

So, she didn't speak up. She never asked for what she needed.

Because she never spoke up and didn't get her needs met in all areas of her life, she shared that she was experiencing energetic overwhelm.

When she thought deeply about it, she could tell it was not what people were not doing for her, it was her having an inner ego struggle about feeling loveable and worthy.

In short, she concluded that the problem wasn't how others were treating her. It wasn't about receiving credit or acknowledgment for her work, her genius. It was all about how she felt about herself.

As she began digging deep into the core issue, she discovered that she truly did feel unlovable and therefore no matter what anyone did or said it did not matter because she did not feel that love within herself.

As we worked together everything began to shift. Her business grew from $650K to over $1.2 million during the pandemic. Her perspective towards her team shifted and they became the most loveable team ever as they were able to expand and take on more work as a team. She deepened her relationship with her husband.

The big piece came when she learned what boundaries meant to her and she put them in place.

Nel learned that boundaries are loving and a way to communicate and collaborate with grace.

Today Nel is speaking up and asking for her needs to be met from the place of truly knowing and believing that she is worthy & loveable.

Setting Boundaries

While some people find setting boundaries straightforward and even enjoy it, many people would rather give in than enter a conversation that might bring about conflict.

Many people, especially women, find it easier to just give in and hope that it all works out. While it's all well and good to want to avoid conflict or difficult conversations, without setting firm boundaries, you'll find that the amount of drama surrounding you and the number of people who are using you will increase.

Setting boundaries is essential for protecting your energy and maintaining your sense of self. Establishing clear boundaries is crucial for maintaining your well-being and asserting your needs. Say no to things that drain your energy or don't align with your values.

Communicate your limits with others and stand firm in them. Remember, you are not obligated to accommodate everyone at the expense of your own comfort and peace of mind. Respecting your own boundaries teaches others to respect them too.

Boundaries are not about being rigid or unapproachable; they are about honoring your needs and ensuring that your relationships are respectful and balanced. By setting and maintaining boundaries, you show others that you value yourself and deserve to be treated with respect.

How many times have you heard the importance of setting strong boundaries for yourself and yet you're still resisting?

Or, perhaps you've set some boundaries only to have people cross the line repeatedly.

Are you ready to set boundaries for yourself or do you believe that they are selfish?

Pay attention to your answer and be honest with yourself. If it's yes, then skip down and I'll share a great formula with you to set and hold boundaries for yourself.

If you answered no, then congratulations for being honest with yourself. Let's spend some time delving into this further. I love the following quote from Louise Hay.

"The only people who get upset about you having boundaries are the ones who were benefiting from you having none." Louise Hay

How does it feel to hear that when you refuse to set boundaries because you don't want to upset someone, it means they are benefiting from you?

Simply put, they are using you.

To be even more dramatic, they are draining your power.

Does this change your mind about setting boundaries for yourself?

If your answer is still no, let's go deeper. Are you concerned about how other people (or a specific person) will feel if you set up some boundaries for yourself? Perhaps you're worried about making them mad. If the other person has been using you and draining your power for years, then, of course, they won't like it and they may not react well the first time. Here's the thing, they know that they are using you. Of course, it's not something that they will admit to readily, deep down, they know they are using you. Often their reaction is because you've changed the terms of the relationship, and they don't like it. Their reaction is because you've finally stood up for yourself. Reasonable people will calm down quickly and come around to your needs. Unreasonable people may decide to go and find someone else to use. It's your decision now if you want this unreasonable person in your life.

If you are still deciding the answer is no, then I have one more thought for you. Do you enjoy having drama in your life? If you do, then the best way to keep the drama going is to not set boundaries. When you set strong and clear boundaries with communication, the drama will disappear.

When you're ready to set strong boundaries and honor yourself, here's how to do it.

To be guided through this powerful technique, follow the video in the Portal via https://millionaire.codes or via the QR code below:

1. When someone asks you for your time or your money or your energy, the first and most important step is to realize **you have a choice** of answering either yes or no. People can only take from you that which you give.

If you've decided no, then tell them. Remember, "no" is a complete sentence. There is no need to explain. If you decide you do want to give a few more words, then just tell them that your focus and priorities are elsewhere and as such, the answer is no. Make sure you don't apologize, there is no need to say sorry.

2. If you've decided you **want to give** to them, then you need to ask yourself if you have it to give. If you don't have the time or money or energy, then you will say no.

If you have the time, money and/or energy, then you can provide the terms of how you want to give to them. Ask yourself what you want to do and how you want to give.

For example, if you own a pickup truck and someone is asking to borrow it to move, then you let them know that they can borrow the truck on a certain day at a certain time and that it must be returned with a full tank of gas by a certain time. Reasonable people will agree to these terms. People who were hoping to use it for as long as they wanted and use your gas will be annoyed. Do you want these people in your life anyway?

3. Now it's time to **outline the consequences**. This is where I find so many people have the most difficult time. If someone has asked you for a favour, then they will treat your time, money and energy just like you will, right? Nope, that's not always the case. They may have other challenges and commitments to deal with and they know that you're always so accommodating, you may be the lesser of their two

evils. So, make sure you objectively set up reasonable consequences if they do not honor their commitment to you.

Going back to the example above, you would let them know that if they don't fill up the tank with gas or there is damage to the truck, you will not lend them anything ever again.

4. Here's the really important part.

You MUST stick to the consequences.

If they don't honor your boundaries, then you must hold the line. This is where people often waffle or give in because it feels too hard to hold the line. If you waffle here, then you'll find setting boundaries a challenge every time. You'll also have much more drama and conflict in your life.

Most people can easily follow the first two steps in setting boundaries: deciding if they have it to give and if they want to give it.

It's the third step that is a bit tricky. How do you know what circumstances or conditions to apply?

Here's the thing, you wouldn't need boundaries if everyone treated you and your belongings the way you want them to, right?

Unfortunately, that's not always the case, is it?

To know the best way to set the circumstances under which you'll provide your time, money, belongings, or energy, you need to go to the worst-case scenario.

What if they don't treat you or your belongings like you want them to?

How do you want them to treat you?

This is the exact reason why we have lawyers who create contracts for each of us.

This is what you're creating when you set a boundary and the circumstances under which you will each behave.

The secret to setting clear boundaries is to go to the worst-case scenario in your head and address all the points that could possibly happen. Then, you can clearly articulate the consequences.

Oh yeah. You must choose to follow through on the consequences.

Yes, this is the uncomfortable part. When you choose to respect and love yourself enough to set strong boundaries, you will have significantly less drama in your life and more respect from others.

So, you have a choice. The first time you set a boundary is the most difficult. It becomes easier and easier every time you do it.

Start with an easy boundary and work your way up. You can do this. Your life will change for the better.

Here's another benefit of setting a loving boundary with a firm consequence, you protect your personal space, your time and your energy.

The Process for Setting Your Boundaries

Step One: External

A boundary needs to be set when someone makes a request for your time, money or energy.

Step Two: Internal

Ask yourself these 3 questions:

1. Do I have it to give? The answer is yes or no. Simple.
2. Do I want to give it? Here's where the choice comes in. Just because someone asks you, doesn't mean you have to give it. What do you want? Be honest with yourself. This is so

important, please remember that others don't get to decide for you. It's up to you to decide.

3. If the answer is yes, under what circumstances or conditions?

Step Three: External

Now it's time for your response.

If the answer is no, it's no. You can respond and tell them no.

Do Not Apologize! Remember, what Louise Hay said, the only people who will be upset about this are the people who are using you. You don't deserve to be used!

If the response is no, just state it simply "no" or "no that won't work for me." That's it.

Just "no" is a simple and complete sentence.

If the answer is yes, remember to be very clear about the conditions and consequences.

When you're clear with the conditions and consequences up front, the drama and conflict will significantly reduce.

You're taking your power back when you set a loving boundary with a firm consequence. You are making sure that your needs are met and getting your needs met is not negotiable. So, next time someone asks you for something, anything, follow the boundary setting process and either say no, without apologizing or yes with specific consequences and conditions.

Millionaire Code 8:
The Integrator

Clare had just made this *huge*, heart-pounding, six-figure investment in her business—a bold move to work with a marketing company that promised to take her visibility to the next level. She was fired up, excited, and ready to go.

But then, that little voice in her head showed up. You know the one. It said, "Who do you think you are? Look at you, thinking you'll be more visible." BAM. Just like that, her excitement was hijacked by doubt.

And then she said something that stopped us both in our tracks: "Part of me wants to hide over here."

That was it. Right there. Her old patterns were creeping in. The part of her that wanted to stay small, to stay safe, was trying to slam on the brakes. It wasn't just fear, it was a deeply ingrained belief that had been holding her back from the visibility and revenue she desired.

We jumped right into The Integrator. It's a simple and powerful process, and let me tell you, what happened next was *amazing*.

In just a few minutes, that negative voice in her head was replaced with something entirely new.

"Remember, you are an amazing investment."

Just like that, Clare flipped the script. She let go of the old pattern and rewired her thinking to fully own her power and potential.

Today, Clare is visible and going for multiple 7 figures in her business. That voice in her head? It's cheering her on.

When you have identified that part of you wants to do one thing and a totally different part of you wants to do another thing, then it's time to use The Integrator. It's time to invite the part or parts to join the whole, your unconscious mind.

The main purpose of The Integrator is to establish and create channels of communication between your unconscious mind and your conscious mind. Remember that all your parts were formed to make sure that your needs were met, and they are all potential teachers and friends.

The parts become a problem when you're not able to make decisions easily because part of you wants one thing and part of you wants another or as previously mentioned, you're behaving incongruently and out of character.

As you engage with and connect with your unconscious mind and the part, you may find that you get different types of signals. You may see images, you may hear sounds or words, you may feel a sensation somewhere in your body. The more you believe that this will work for you and that your unconscious mind is able to communicate with you, the more this will work for you.

You can either read through the process below, or go to the Millionaire Codes Portal via https://millionaire.codes or via the QR code below:

Let's get started:

1. What behaviors, feelings or responses are you experiencing part of the time that make you cringe?
2. Has someone ever said to you that you were behaving like a kid?
3. What action or actions are you not able to take easily?
4. What decisions are you waffling about making?

Answering these questions will give you clues on what patterns of behavior you're experiencing that may be initiated by a stuck part in your unconscious mind.

Identify the behavior that you want to change. Move to a place where you can close your eyes and begin to connect with your unconscious mind.

Relax and turn within. Breathe deeply, in and out.

1. Recall a specific time when you displayed the behavior that you are seeking to change. You may see images or have different sensations or hear something. However you do this is perfect. Simply relax and pay attention to what comes up for you.
2. Now, ask the part in charge of behavior if it's willing to communicate. See what image, sound, word, sensation comes up for you when asking that question. Ask the part to increase that image, sound, sensation if answer is yes and decrease if answer is no.
3. Thank the part for communicating and reassure the part that it is entirely understandable that it may not want to communicate on a conscious level. Reassure the part that it is in charge of the behavior and in no way are you trying to get rid of it, we are only trying to get some information and congruency.
4. Ask the part what it's highest purpose or positive intention is. The part may answer consciously or unconsciously. Know that

the part will always have a positive intention. Imagine what the deeply positive purpose or intention of this part may be. The purpose here is to separate behavior from intention or function and to get your conscious mind to begin to appreciate that part as friend and/or teacher.

Thank the part for positive intention and sincerely appreciate the part.

5. Now it's time to go to the creative part in your unconscious mind and ask that it generate at least three (3) alternatives to the behavior that is not serving you that would satisfy the part's positive intention or highest purpose but in a different way. These new choices can be on a conscious level. Simply ask your creative part to give you a signal when it has generated these three (3) new alternatives.

Thank the creative part.

6. Ask the part responsible for the behavior that you want to change whether it's willing to use these alternative choices instead of the behavior(s). You'll get a yes or a no signal.

a. If yes, thank the part and go on.

b. If no, put a time limit on request (e.g., 2 weeks, etc.) to try out some alternatives to find out if they are effective and available.

c. If still no, ask part to go back to the creative part and help generate alternatives it would be willing to try out for at least a limited time.

Thank the part.

7. Ecological check. Check with all your parts to make sure all are comfortable and accept the entire process and the alternatives.

a. If yes, thank all the parts and surprise and delight yourself in future.

b. If no, check on how you know this, how this represents an objection, then ask the image, sound, sensation, and increase if needed. Any objection is important information and is welcome. If there is an objection, go back to step #3 and go through the process with the part that objects - making sure that the objecting part and the part that runs the behavior you want to change agree on all the alternatives and can work together. Treat the parts as though they were all parts of a negotiating team. It is important that each member's function and purpose be respected and paid attention to. Cycle back through the process until you get full acceptance for any alternative behaviors from all parts involved.

Thank all the parts.

Millionaire Code 9:
The Destiny Maker

"Decisions determine our destiny"
—Tony Robbins

Ah decisions. As thought leaders, coaches, healers, experts, entrepreneurs, parents, partners, global citizens, we're asked to make decisions every day.

Are decisions easy for you? If you're like most people, and according to the stakes of the decision, you don't find this easy. In fact, according to a 2023 study – The Decision Dilemma – by Oracle and Seth Stephens-Davidowitz, New York Times bestselling author where 14,000 employees and business leaders across 17 countries participated found that people are struggling to make decisions in their personal and professional lives at a time when they are being forced to make more decisions than ever before. 70% of adults in 2024 reported they would rather have a robot make their decisions for them!

Thankfully, today Suzanne and I are not in that 70% and after activating this code, we affirm you won't be either, let's give ourselves some compassion! Science has demonstrated that we make 35,000 conscious decisions PER DAY! 35,000! That's a lot to ask from anyone. This creates understandable anxiety and the "decision fatigue" that had American President Obama fill his closet with rows of matching gray suits, so he never had to choose what to wear. This is also the reason why Magic 8 Balls are still on the market.

Big decisions. You know the ones I'm talking about—do I make this investment? Take the trip? Buy the house? Marry the person? Launch the program? Hire the team member? Leave the position? Spend the money on marketing? We pile on the pressure, don't we? We know these decisions matter, and the stakes feel high.

Experts throw phrases at us like "money loves speed" and "great leaders decide quickly," and yet here we are, stuck in the loop of overthinking. Is it the *right* decision? We agonize, weighing every angle. And let's be honest—our brains are wired to focus on what we might lose instead of what we could gain. Especially women. We think about the cost—money, time, energy—and what happens if it doesn't pay off. We spiral into *what ifs*. What if we fail? What if it's public? What if we can't come back from it?

Let me cut to the chase: you can't know. Not completely. There are no guarantees. That's life. Every decision involves some level of risk. But here's the good news: you *can* make decisions that are powerful, accurate, and aligned with your mission. That's why I developed what I call the Millionaire Code.

I've used this code for every big decision I've made in the past five years. It's helped me, and I've taught it to over 1,000 entrepreneurs, authors, moms, clients, and friends at my Bestselling Book Bootcamp. And let me tell you, writing a book? It's basically a masterclass in decision-making!

If you want to do the extended code along with us, head to the Portal and access the video for this code via https://millionaire.codes or via the QR code below:

Our vision is you'll start to enjoy making decisions- even get excited to decide because you'll know you have a way to access your highest intuition, wisdom and the guidance of the Universe.

Whenever I get nervous to make a decision, I think of the fabulous W.H. Murray quote.

> "Until one is committed, there is hesitancy, the chance to draw back. Concerning all acts of initiative (and creation), there is one elementary truth, the ignorance of which kills countless ideas and splendid plans: that the moment one definitely commits oneself, then Providence moves too. All sorts of things occur to help one that would never otherwise have occurred. A whole stream of events issues from the decision, raising in one's favor all manner of unforeseen incidents and meetings and material assistance, which no man could have dreamed would have come his way. Whatever you can do, or dream you can do, begin it. Boldness has genius, power, and magic in it. Begin it now."
>
> — *W.H. Murray*

You deserve to live in boldness, genius and magic- so let's activate this code!

To do this, follow the video in the Portal via https://millionaire.codes or via the QR code below:

Preparation: 1 piece of paper + something to write with (works best to write vs type.)

Step 1

Write the thing you want, clarity around - the decision you want to make - at the top of a piece of paper.

Then: say out loud to yourself: *I already know the answer.*

This happens to be true, but even if you don't believe it, speaking this will prime your brain to bring your answer during this code activation.

Step 2:

On the left side of your paper, write the top three reasons not to do this thing (in other words, to decide "no".)

On the right, you'll write the top three reasons to do it (decide "yes".)

Just be curious.

Example:

Reasons not to write the book I'm considering:

Will take a lot of time

Don't know if people will like it/read it

Costs money to work with an editor/publisher

Reason to write the book I'm considering:

I feel high passion for this idea and if I do it well, I think it would help a lot of people

I would have fun researching and immersing in this topic

3 signs from Universe in the last week that point toward me doing something on this topic

I write my two lists, and then again, with curiosity, I analyze them. What I'm looking for, personally, is clues as to which parts of me are invested in doing it or not doing it. Bottom line, I'm looking for what's fear and what's intuitive guidance.

In this example, the first list sounds like scarcity: time, money and also external validation: will people like it. Those are all valid things to consider, but there's an undercurrent of fear.

On the right, I hear soul, passion, universe, calling, service.

I compare the lists by what I value most. Because I've made a commitment to live from vision versus fear and I value calling and service, this one suggests to me a "yes." However, don't make a decision yet. Make your two lists, explore how they relate to your values, and then move to the next step in the code.

Step 3

For this final step of the process, you'll want to stand up a little bit of space out in front, to the left, and out in front to the right of you. If you're not in a space where you can physically do this. You can envision yourself doing the movements I describe. Bringing the body into this can be so powerful. Your mind, your subconscious, your higher self, already know the answer, and so does your body.

Your starting spot in the middle is neutral.

Call the decision you want to make to your mind.

Assign to the front and left of you as you NOT doing the thing, a "no" decision. To the front right is DOING it, a "yes" decision.

Take a few deep breaths, grounding and centering yourself in neutral, and then, with curiosity, step front and left into the path where you decided not to do this thing. Take your time with this, and again, you can go to the Portal via https://millionaire.codes or via the QR code below and do this with us so you don't have to read and do this at the same time.

Step fully into the front left position where you've made the choice of not doing this thing. It's a way down the road and you've decided not to do it. Close your eyes.

First, notice any physical sensations.

Next, notice any emotions that arise from having chosen the path of not doing this.

Now, notice what's happening in your life, having not made this decision. Who are you with? How do you feel about yourself? What's happening in your relationships, your bank account. What's on your calendar?

Tune into any other guidance about you having not made this decision.

Then, with a big breath, step back to your neutral spot in the middle.

Feel a rain shower of light, balancing and centering you.

Now count to three and step to the front right where you decided TO do this thing. Just like on the left:

Notice any physical sensations.

Next, notice any emotions that arise from having chosen the path of doing this.

Now, notice what's happening in your life, having made this decision. Who are you with? How do you feel about yourself? What's happening in your relationships, your bank account? What's on your calendar?

Tune into any other guidance about you having made this choice and taken this path.

Then, with a big breath, step back to your neutral spot in the middle.

Feel a rain shower of light, balancing and centering you.

Gently and lovingly, bring yourself fully back into full focus.

Take a few minutes to write what you observed between the two paths.

One of our clients, Melanie, did this, and couldn't believe the difference she felt physically. On the left, she felt this swirling, kind of chaotic energy. She felt contracted. Her body was leaning forward. On the right, she felt peaceful, expansive, confident. This contrast gave her peace that doing the thing was right to her, even though she was scared.

Other times, I've seen clients jump back after stepping into the right spot and say, "Nope, I know I don't want that!" Quite often, people don't want to step back from the direction that feels the best. They become more excited and "bought in" to their ideal path. Clarity is always a gift. So whether we're getting led to do something or not, the clarity is something to be celebrated.

The final piece of this code is to bring yourself back to the statement, *I already know the answer.*

Take a fresh piece of paper. Write: I already know the answer and the answer is: _____ [fill in your clearest answer based on what came through in the code.]

If you're not completely clear yet, that's fine! You can use the code several times.

When more clarity is needed, I continue to meditate, to journal, to talk to mentors, to vision quest.

Here's my ultimate SUPERSIZE move for this code. I say:

"I make a decision, and I make it the right decision."

You have this agency. You have this power! You decide and then YOU make it the "right" decision.

Saying this doesn't mean everything goes according to our initial vision, but by reminding yourself of your own power, your own agency, that you get to make something the right decision.

If you make an investment and it seems like it's not going the best way, how do you turn that into a powerful opportunity? Yes, for learning and growth, sure, but literally, how do you leverage it? How do you leverage it and make it an opportunity?

Earlier this year, one of my clients took on a massive project. From the start, it was rough. It was stressful, way more work than she expected, and to top it off, she felt like she undercharged. Then, the client brought in a new partner who hired *their own coach*, so there went any future income from the deal. She was beating herself up, convinced she'd made the wrong decision.

I showed her this code, just this last part. She told herself; "*I make a decision and MAKE it the right decision.*"

I asked her, "What would it look like to leverage this experience and turn it into a great decision?" She said, "Well, I'd need to see a big financial return." I responded with, "Great! What would it take to create that big return?"

At first, she hit me with all the reasons why it *couldn't* happen. The client had moved on, she'd sunk way more hours than planned, and she was done with the project. But then something clicked. She realized that most people in her industry approach these kinds of projects in a super inefficient way—spending way more time and money than necessary. That's when the light bulb went off.

She decided to create a new offer that streamlined the process and gave everyone involved a win. This new offer is now part of her business suite, and it has the potential to bring in exponential income. What started as a stressful, "wrong" decision became the foundation for something that could help her make money *again and again and again.*

Here's the truth: the best decisions aren't the ones without challenges—they're the ones you decide to make great. That's where the magic is.

From now on, you make a decision, and then you make it the right one. You've got this!

Millionaire Code 10:
The Manifestor

Use this code when you know what you want but crave more conviction, clarity, and belief in your goal becoming reality.

This is your go-to code for blasting through imposter syndrome, fear, doubt, worry, distraction, procrastination, and resistance. It's like flipping a switch—turning hesitation into momentum and uncertainty into unstoppable action.

There was a day I woke up feeling stress and anxiety because I was very clear on the next big vision that I wanted to manifest: hitting the bestseller list with my upcoming book. I knew the vision, but I worried that it would never happen.

These thoughts were running on repeat in my head: "You haven't done this before. You don't know what you're doing. Who do you think you are anyway?"

These gremlin thoughts were frustrating because I know better. I know that the best thing we can do is focus on vision- acting as if it's already done, generating those faith-filled, positive feelings.

But I couldn't get there.

Instead of actually developing a strategy or getting more support, or doing anything constructive, I kept looping in fear, worry, anxiety and shame.

I wanted to BELIEVE in the vision. To keep my thoughts focused on the positive outcome. I wanted something to line up my VIBRATION with the fulfillment of this vision.

We developed this code to help you do exactly this: align, embody and ACTIVATE yourself into the reality of the vision fulfilled and let this lead you to empowered action.

I've used it to manifest health goals, parenting goals, 5 bestselling books and millions of dollars.

Let's GOOO!

Note: This code requires some materials, so we recommend you read through the process first and then take yourself through the code.

First: assemble 5 post-it notes or index cards.

Label the cards this way:

-5
C
M1
M2
V

Write your big goal on one of the cards/post-its. Example: Bestseller List, TEDx talk, $100,000.

Next, on a separate piece of paper, identify two milestones a person would reach on the way to that goal. My favorite question to ask here is "what would let you know you are on your way to manifestation of this big vision? What happens along the way that demonstrates you're in process, you're moving closer, it's in motion?

So for example if you set a financial goal of $100,000 in the next 90 days, one milestone might be $35K at 30 and then hitting $70K at 60 days. The 30 days with income jumps would be your two big milestones. In my example of reaching the bestseller list, the milestones would be M1: finishing the manuscript! At M2: the publisher would be creating the cover design, preparing for launch and I would be in action, speaking on podcasts, connecting with influencers and potential readers on social media and giving great value to them, nurturing those relationships and building awareness for the book so they would genuinely be excited to read and share when it came out.

Now, moving backwards, contemplate your current reality. What is going on right now in your life in relation to your goal? In my case of the first bestseller the current reality was waking up worried that I would not make the list. In the current state, I compared myself to other writers and thought leaders who were bestsellers and feared I would never be one of them. I spent more time concerned with future outcomes than actually taking action towards developing relationships or building an audience of people that would be interested in the book.

Once you have these coordinates clear, set the cards/post-its on the floor in front of you in a vertical line with -5 being the closest to you and V being the furthest from you.

You can read through this and then do the code OR if you want to be guided through this so you can have the experience vs try and read while doing the code, enter the Portal via https://millionaire.codes or via the QR code.

Stand on the card labeled "C."

This is your current reality. As you stand on C, completely immerse yourself in what has been happening now in relation to your big vision. Imagine you're watching a movie of how life has been around this goal. See what you are doing or not doing, who you are with, how that is affecting all the areas of your life like self-esteem, relationships, finances, purpose etc. Then, very importantly, notice how you FEEL in this reality.

Take a huge, big breath (you're doing great!)

Then step forward to the card labeled M1. Just like you did for the current state, immerse yourself in this first milestone.

You've taken certain actions and you're seeing signs of progress that you are moving toward your vision. What signs are you seeing that you are moving forward on your path?

Once again, imagine you're watching a movie of yourself at this first milestone. See what you are doing or not doing, who you are with, how that is affecting all the areas of your life like self-esteem, relationships, finances, purpose etc. Then, very importantly, notice how you FEEL at this progress point.

Take another big breath (keep up the great work!)

Now move forward to M2. You've reached another great milestone that lets you know you have made even more progress on your vision. Envision what you are doing or not doing, who you are with, how that is affecting all the areas of your life like self-esteem, relationships, finances, purpose etc. Then, very importantly, notice how you FEEL at this progress point.

Big breath!

Now joyfully step to the card marked "V." This is where the full vision has happened! You did it! Everything that you set out to do you have accomplished and it is now your new reality. What's amazing, better and different in your life now that you've accomplished and manifested this big dream?

What is the #1 biggest feeling you feel when this is your new reality-your new life?

Spend some wonderful time dialing up the predominant feelings (satisfaction, joy, gratitude, awe, relief.)

Breathe deeply.

Now, go back and stand on the "C" card.

Anchor yourself in the current reality. Notice whatever comes up for you. Do you feel resistance to coming all the way back? Do you want to quickly jump back forward towards your vision? Do you feel comfortable at C?

Move from C, M1, M2 and V two more times. Do the same visualizing + feeling for each state.

Now, stand on "C" and take a breath.

Being careful, step backwards onto -5.

You are now in the reality of you 5 years ago. Take yourself back to what was happening in your life 5 years prior. Where were you? Who were you with? What was the state of your relationships, personal growth, spirituality, finances, work life and personal life?

What do you notice? How do you feel standing in you 5 years ago? Pay attention to any strong feelings or awarenesses that arise.

Now share with the you from 5 years ago all that's happened between where she is and "C." Give her a hug and thank her for getting you that far so you could continue your journey. Take a breath and move back to "C."

How does it feel to be back in your current reality? Notice and then step, jump or skip forward to M1. Now M2. And then V.

Move from C to V either once or a few more times (your intuition will tell you how many rounds to do.)

By cycling from C to V, you're solidifying the pathway into your subconscious and creating an inevitable arrival at your vision. You learned in Part I that the subconscious mind does not know the difference between imagination and reality. Your subconscious mind is like a sponge—it gets reprogrammed through repetition and imagery. Every time you step into those milestones and see your vision as *already done*, you're not just daydreaming—you're *locking in* the reality of your vision.

Carl Jung had it right, when he said, *"Until you make the unconscious conscious, it will direct your life, and you will call it fate."* That's exactly what's happening here. By doing this code, you're making your vision so familiar that it feels like second nature. You've been here before. You've already done it. And that? That's where the magic starts to happen.

As you cycle through the steps, pay attention to any new details or ideas that rise in your mind. Sometimes, clients I take through this code get intuitive flashes of people to reach out to, actions steps to take. Often, your M1 and M2s will clarify, crystalize and magnetize.

When I used this code that day on my vision of becoming a bestselling author, I started to feel excited about the next steps.

I started to think of people who said to let them know when the book was coming out and I made a list of those who might be interested in sharing with their audiences if I sent them an advanced copy of the book.

In M2 I saw myself writing a press release. I'd never written one but when I finished doing this code, I did a quick google search later and in seconds, I had a template. I'd seen myself connecting with influencers so after the code, I scrolled through social media and made a list of 100 people that looked interested in my book topic. I felt nervous at the idea of contacting them but I'd just seen myself do it in M2 so I made a commitment to reach out to every one of them.

While nothing seemed to change in my current reality, I did notice that my energy and focus was now on action and excitement was the primary emotion. I used what came through in that code to develop a bestseller launch plan that has now helped thousands of experts and coaches to hit the bestseller list with their books.

We're SO excited for you to use this code on your BIG VISION! Bonus: take a picture of yourself walking the C to V path. Access the Portal via https://millionaire.codes or via the QR code below.

We'll be envisioning you at V now!

One More Surprise

Alright, let's talk about what just happened here. You've taken a journey—a *big* one—through the conscious and subconscious layers of your mind. As you've released those old stories of lack and scarcity, you've activated the 10 Millionaire Codes and set a *completely new trajectory* for your financial future. No, scratch that—your *destiny*.

Yes, destiny.

This isn't just about money. This is about stepping into the life you were *always* meant to live.

Let's summarize:

We wrote this book during an era of a different epidemic. No, not COVID—it's something sneakier, something that's been around longer: the epidemic of fear, lack, and self-doubt. The kind that keeps women playing small, shrinking back, and believing they're not enough.

Here's the crazy part: by reading this book, you've done something extraordinary. You've rewritten your energetic DNA. (Yes, you read that right—energetic DNA.) And here's what makes this even *wilder*: through the magic of epigenetics, we've explored how fear, trauma, and scarcity from generations before you are literally passed down in your genes. But here's the thing—the Millionaire Codes? They're here to clear all that. They align you with your *true nature* so you can finally be free to have, do, and become *everything* you've ever desired.

But wait—it gets better. Because what we tested wasn't just epigenetics. No, we went even deeper. Deeper than your past. Deeper than your ancestors. We tapped into something that has *always* been part of you.

It's called **The Millionaire Gene**. Simply turn the page to see your results.

Genetic
TESTING CENTER

Here are your test results...

TESTED GENE: **LUX1-$$**
TEST RESULT: **Positive for the Millionaire Gene**

GENE DESCRIPTION:
The LUX1-$$, commonly referred to as the Millionaire Gene, is a unique genetic marker associated with extraordinary financial acumen and wealth accumulation capabilities. This gene has been linked to key personality traits such as exceptional entrepreneurship, global thought leadership and industry leadership.

SYMPTOMS:

- **Increased Financial Intuition:** An uncanny ability to predict profitable ventures well before they become mainstream.

- **Enhanced Money-Making Skills:** Whether it's negotiating deals or spotting market trends, carriers of the LUX1-$$ gene are naturals at increasing their net worth.

- **Luxury Affinity:** A natural attraction to quality and luxury, often accompanied by an intuitive understanding of the true value of objects.

- **Charismatic Leadership:** The ability to inspire and lead in business environments, often resulting in successful entrepreneurial endeavors.

TREATMENT:
As this gene enhances your innate abilities to generate and attract wealth, the recommended treatment involves embracing your potential:

- **Development:** investing in experiences that increase your frequency, expand your abundance channel and Raise you into your greatness.

- **Networking:** Expand your social circle to include fellow visionaries and multi-millionaires to raise your vibration and stretch you to new heights.

- **Mindset:** Taking time to visualize, generate emotions and increase passion for your vision will pull your vision into 3D form.

- **Prosperous Purchasing:** Circulating and investing in experiences and purchases that are a vibrational match to the future vision will accelerate manifestation.

PROGNOSIS:
With the right mindset and application, individuals testing positive for the LUX1-$$ gene have a high probability of achieving massive financial success and life purpose fulfillment. Embrace your destiny as a future multi-millionaire!

Now you know your truth. You have it. The Millionaire Gene. Of course, you do!

You were *always* meant for this.

You've got it in your DNA to be a millionaire—heck, a *multi-millionaire.*

It's who you are.

It's your birthright.

The only thing left to do is make it *real.*

Move it from the 5D quantum field to the 3D physical world.

It's your time. *Now.*

And here's why this matters so much: when you rise, you lift others with you. As Marianne Williamson says, *"You're not broke; you're just pre-rich."* When you step into your power, your wealth, your *true identity*, you inspire every other woman around you to do the same. Your playing small has *never* served anyone.

And your rise? It's a gift to the world.

As the Dalai Lama said, *"The world will be saved by the Western woman,"* and by stepping into your wealth, power, and purpose, you're not just transforming your life—you're becoming part of a global movement to change the world for the better.

So thank you.

Thank you for saying yes to your destiny.

Thank you for not just increasing your own wealth, but for lifting the wealth, confidence, and freedom of women everywhere.

This is how we change the world—one bold, unapologetic step at a time. Now go. Make it real. Let's GO!

Glossary of Terms

Accountability Partner/Accountability Buddy

A trusted individual or peer who holds space as a witness in sharing big dreams and goals. They offer encouragement and help someone stay on track toward achieving their goals. This relationship keeps the individual accountable for their own actions and celebrates wins with enthusiasm.

Amygdala

An almond-shaped part of the brain's limbic system that processes emotions like fear, anger, and stress. It plays a key role in triggering the fight, flight, or freeze response and storing emotional memories.

Anchors

Physical or mental cues associated with a particular emotional or mental state.

Anchoring

A technique used in NLP to associate a physical or mental trigger with a desired emotional state, enabling quick access to empowering emotions.

Beliefs

Generalized interpretations about the world, often formed in early life, that shape perceptions and actions.

Complex PTSD (C-PTSD)

A condition often experienced by individuals subjected to prolonged trauma, addressed through NLP techniques in the book.

Ecology

Ecology refers to the alignment of goals, actions, and outcomes with a person's values, well-being, and the broader impact on others. It ensures that changes or decisions are beneficial and sustainable for the individual and their environment.

Emotional Resilience

The ability to recover quickly from emotional setbacks and maintain mental clarity and balance.

Gestalt

A pattern in the unconscious mind that organizes memories and emotions into a cohesive whole, influencing reactions and behavior.

Gremlins

Internal, critical voices or negative thought patterns that undermine confidence and reinforce limiting beliefs. These "gremlins" are often rooted in past experiences and can be addressed using NLP techniques to shift mindset and behaviors.

Lion's Breath

A yoga breathing technique involving a deep inhale and a forceful exhale with an open mouth, tongue out, and a "HA!" sound. It releases tension, reduces stress, and boosts energy.

Meta Programs

Hidden patterns or mental filters that guide how people think, decide, and act.

Millionaire Codes

A series of ten transformational sequences designed to ignite personal and professional potential, focusing on mindset shifts and rewiring the brain for success.

Neuro-Linguistic Programming (NLP)

A method blending psychology, neuroscience, hypnosis, and communication techniques to help rewire the brain for desired outcomes by shifting thoughts, emotions, and behaviors.

Neurology (in NLP)

Refers to the brain and nervous system's role in processing thoughts, emotions, and behaviors. Changing your neurology means rewiring the pathways in your brain to create new habits, beliefs, and responses, ultimately leading to personal transformation and success.

Neurotransmitters

Chemical messengers in the brain and nervous system that transmit signals between neurons. They play a key role in regulating mood, behavior, memory, and bodily functions.

Parts Integration

An NLP method for resolving internal conflicts by uniting different aspects of the unconscious mind.

Perception is Projection

Principle stating that how individuals interpret the world is a reflection of their internal beliefs and thoughts, not objective reality.

Presuppositions of NLP

Core beliefs underlying NLP, such as "There is no failure, only feedback," and "The map is not the territory," emphasizing adaptability and personal interpretation.

Quantum Thinking

The concept that thoughts and beliefs operate at a quantum level, influencing reality. This ties into the idea of shifting perspectives to affect outcomes.

Reframing

The process of changing the meaning of an experience or thought to see it in a more positive or empowering way.

Reticular Activating System (RAS)

A network of neurons in the brainstem that filters sensory information and determines what gets your attention. The RAS helps focus on what is most important, aligning with your goals and beliefs, and plays a key role in perception and awareness.

Subconscious/Unconscious Mind

The part of the mind that operates below conscious awareness, storing habits, beliefs, and memories that influence behavior and perception. Often used interchangeably in the book.

Timeline Therapy™ Techniques

A technique for clearing negative emotions and limiting beliefs by addressing their root causes in the unconscious mind.

The Universal Law of Causality

A philosophical and scientific principle stating that every effect has a cause, used in this context to highlight personal responsibility for outcomes.

Values

Deep-seated beliefs acting as an internal compass, guiding decisions and judgments about right and wrong in various life contexts.

Visualization

A mental technique involving vividly imagining specific scenarios or outcomes to create positive associations and influence real-life results.